level X

PAUL GALLICO

FLOWERS
FOR MRS HARRIS

Simplified and abridged by
R.H. Durham

Longman

Longman Group UK Limited,
Longman House, Burnt Mill, Harlow,
Essex CM20 2JE, England
and Associated Companies throughout the world.

First published in this series
by arrangement with Messrs Michael Joseph Ltd 1964
This impression 1993

Produced by Longman Singapore Publishers Pte Ltd
Printed in Singapore

ISBN 0-582-53024-5

THE BRIDGE SERIES

The *Bridge Series* is intended for students of English as a second or foreign language who have progressed beyond the elementary graded readers and the *Longman Simplified English Series* but are not yet sufficiently advanced to read works of literature in their original form.

The books in the *Bridge Series* are moderately simplified in vocabulary and often slightly reduced in length, but with little change in syntax. The purpose of the texts is to give practice in understanding fairly advanced sentence patterns and to help in the appreciation of English style. We hope that they will prove enjoyable to read for their own sake and that they will at the same time help students to reach the final objective of reading original works of literature in English with full understanding and appreciation.

Technical Note

The vocabulary of the *Simplified English Series* is the 2,000 words of the *General Service List* (*Interim Report on Vocabulary Selection*) and there is a degree of structure control. In the *Bridge Series* words outside the commonest 7,000 (in Thorndike and Lorge: *A Teacher's Handbook of 30,000 Words*, Columbia University, 1944) have usually been replaced by commoner and more generally useful words. Words used which are outside the first 3,000 of the list are explained in a glossary and are so distributed throughout the book that they do not occur at a greater density than 25 per running 1,000 words.

Introduction

The author of this book, Paul Gallico, was born in New
York City in 1897. Not long after leaving Columbia
University in New York, he served in the United States
Navy in the First World War. From 1922 until 1936 he
was a member of the staff of the *New York Daily News* as
sports editor and as a columnist writing articles for his own
column in the newspaper.

Paul Gallico, whose name was already familiar to readers
of magazines on both sides of the Atlantic, became known
in many other parts of the world after the publication in
1941 of his story of the retreat through Dunkirk, *The Snow
Goose*. In 1944 he became a war correspondent with the
American forces.

Readers may since then have seen films whose stories
were written by Paul Gallico. He has also written short
stories and several novels, among the latter *Mrs Harris
Goes to New York* (1960), another story about the lovable
character in this book. Among his serious works are *The
Steadfast Man* (1958), which studies the life of St Patrick,
and *The Hurricane Story* (1959) about the famous British
fighter-planes of the Second World War.

Flowers for Mrs Harris, published in 1958, is the tender
little story of a dream and its outcome. It takes us from
London to Paris and back again to London—or does it take
us to fairyland and back?

Mrs Harris is a 'daily', a London charwoman who, for

three shillings an hour, cleans and tidies other people's houses. She has one great ambition: she must buy a dress from the most famous dressmakers in the world, The House of Dior in Paris. After three years of hard work and desperate saving we follow her to Paris. Why should the reader, or the gods and goddesses on the staff of The House of Dior, care whether this odd little woman realizes her dream or not? It must be because Mrs Harris is so very human; being human herself, she assumes that the gods and goddesses are human, and treats them accordingly. The money she has saved may buy her the wonderful dress; money is not concerned in the true result of her trip to Paris. Back in London once more, she discovers that she will never again feel lonely and unwanted.

British currency was changed to Decimal Currency on 15 February, 1971.

Chapter 1

The small, slender woman with apple-red cheeks, greying hair, and sharp little eyes sat with her face pressed against the cabin window of the BEA Viscount on the morning flight from London to Paris. As, with a rush and a roar it lifted itself from the ground, her spirits rose with it. She was nervous, but not at all frightened, for she was convinced that nothing could happen to her now. Hers was the happiness of one who knew that at last she was off upon the adventure at the end of which lay her heart's desire.

She was neatly dressed in a somewhat shabby brown coat and clean brown cotton gloves, and she carried an old imitation leather brown handbag which she held close to her. And this was wise, for it contained not only ten one-pound notes, the legal limit of currency that could be exported from the British Isles, and a return air ticket to Paris, but also the sum of fourteen hundred dollars in American currency, a thick roll of five, ten and twenty-dollar bills, held together by a rubber band. Only in the hat she wore did her high-spirited nature reveal itself. It was of green straw and to the front of it was attached the stem of a huge imitation rose.

Any London housewife who had ever employed the services of those wonderful 'daily women', who come in to scrub and tidy up by the hour, would have said: 'The woman under that hat could only be a London char,' and what is more, they would have been right.

On the Viscount's passenger list she appeared as Mrs. Ada Harris, No. 5, Willis Gardens, Battersea, London S.W. 11, and she was indeed a charwoman, and a widow.

Up to that magic moment of finding herself lifted off the face of the earth her life had been one of never-ending toil, relieved by nothing more than an occasional visit to the pictures, or the pub on the corner.

The world in which Mrs. Harris, now approaching her sixties, moved, was one of continual dirt, and untidiness. Not once, but half a dozen times a day she opened the doors of homes or flats with the keys entrusted to her, to face the dirty dishes and greasy pans in the kitchen, un-made beds, clothing scattered about, wet towels on the bathroom floor, water left in the tooth-glass, dirty clothes to be packed up and, of course, cigarette ends in the ash-trays, dust on tables and mirrors, and all the other dirt that human pigs are capable of leaving behind them when they leave their homes in the morning.

Mrs. Harris cleaned up these places because it was her profession, a way of making a living and keeping body and soul together. And yet, with some chars there was more to it than just that, and particularly with Mrs. Harris – a kind of continual house-proudness, something in which a person might take pride and satisfaction. She came to these rooms to find them pigsties, she left them neat, clean, sparkling and sweet-smelling. The fact that when she returned the next day they would be pigsties all over again, did not bother her. She was paid her fifteen pence an hour and she would leave them spotless. This was the life and profession of the little woman, one of thirty passengers on the plane for Paris.

The green and brown map of British soil slipped beneath

the wings of the airplane and gave way suddenly to the blue of the English Channel, and for the first time Mrs. Harris realised that she was leaving England behind her and was about to enter a foreign country, to be amongst foreign people who spoke a foreign language and who, from all she had ever heard about them, were immoral, greedy, ate frogs, and were particularly inclined to crimes of passion. She was still not afraid, for fear has no place in the vocabulary of the British char, but she was now all the more determined to be on her guard and not allow any nonsense. It was a tremendous purpose that was taking her to Paris, but she hoped in the accomplishing of it to have as little to do with the French people as possible.

They landed smoothly at the French airport and Mrs. Harris's spirits rose still further. None of her friend Mrs. Butterfield's gloomy fears that the thing would either blow up in the sky or plunge with her to the bottom of the sea had come true. Paris perhaps might not prove so frightening after all. Nevertheless, from now on she was inclined to be suspicious and careful, a feeling not lessened by the long bus ride from Le Bourget Airport through strange streets, lined with strange houses and shops offering strange goods in a strange language.

The British European Airways man whose duty was to assist travellers confused by the strangeness of the Invalides Air Station in Paris took one look at the hat, the bag, the large shoes and, of course, sharp almost naughty little eyes, and recognised her immediately for what she was. 'Good Heavens!' he said to himself under his breath, 'a London char! What on earth is she doing here in Paris?'

He noted her uncertainty, quickly glanced at his list and guessed right again. Moving smoothly to her side he

4

touched his cap and asked: 'Can I help you in any way, Mrs. Harris?'

The clever, sharp eyes looked at him carefully. Somewhat to her disappointment he seemed just like any Englishman. Since his approach was polite and harmless, she said cautiously, 'Oh, so they can speak English over here.'

The Airways man said: 'Well, ma'am, I ought to, I *am* British. But I think you will find most people over here speak a little English and you can manage. I see you are returning with us on the eleven o'clock plane this evening. Is there any particular place you wish to go now?'

Mrs. Harris reflected upon just how much she was prepared to tell a stranger and then replied firmly: 'I'll just have a taxi. I've got my ten pounds.'

'Ah, well then,' the Airways man continued, 'you'd better have some of it in French money. One pound comes to roughly a thousand francs.'

At the bureau de change a few of Mrs. Harris's green pound notes were translated into thousand franc notes and hundred franc coins. Then the Airways man placed her in a taxi. 'Where shall I tell him to take you?'

Mrs. Harris sat up with her slender back, thin from hard work, absolutely straight, the pink rose pointing due north, her face as calm as that of a noblewoman. Only the little eyes were dancing with excitement. 'Tell him to take me to the dress shop of Christian Dior,' she said.

The Airways man stared at her, refusing the evidence of his ears. 'I beg your pardon, ma'am?'

'The dress shop of Dior, you heard me!'

The Airways man had heard her all right, but his brain, used to dealing with all kind of emergencies and queer cases, just could not grasp the connection between a London

5

daily woman, one of that vast army that went out every morning to scrub up the City's dirt in office and home, and the most exclusive fashion centre in the world, and he still hesitated.

'Come on then, get on with it,' commanded Mrs. Harris sharply, 'what's so strange about a lady going to buy herself a dress in Paris?'

Shaken with amazement the Airways man spoke to the driver in French: 'Take madame to the House of Christian Dior in the Avenue Montaigne.'

As Mrs. Harris was driven off he went back inside shaking his head. He felt he had seen everything now.

Riding along in the taxi, her heart beating with excitement, Mrs. Harris's thoughts went back to London and she hoped that Mrs. Butterfield would be able to manage.

In Mrs. Harris's list of clients, there were some to whom she gave several hours every day and others who desired her services only three times a week. She worked ten hours a day, her labours beginning at eight in the morning and ending at six o'clock in the night with a half-day devoted to certain favoured customers on Saturdays. This time-table she maintained fifty-two weeks in the year. Since there were just so many hours in a day her patrons were limited to some six or eight.

There was a Major Wallace, her bachelor in whose frequent and changing love affairs she took an eager interest.

She was fond of Mrs. Schreiber, the somewhat vague-minded wife of a Hollywood film representative living in London, for her American warmth and generosity, which displayed itself in many ways, but chiefly by her interest in and consideration for Mrs. Harris.

She worked for fashionable Lady Dant, the wife of a wealthy industrialist, who maintained a flat in London as well as a country house.

There were others, including a little actress, Miss Pamela Penrose, who was struggling to gain recognition in the theatre. All of these establishments Mrs. Harris looked after quite on her own. Yet in an emergency she could fall back on her friend, Mrs. Violet Butterfield, like herself a widow and a char, and inclined to take the gloomy view of life and affairs wherever there was any choice.

Mrs. Butterfield, who was as large and stout as Mrs. Harris appeared to be thin and frail, naturally had her own set of clients, fortunately in the same neighbourhood. But they helped one another whenever the necessity arose.

If either of them was ill or had pressing business elsewhere, the other would manage to take enough time from her clients to make the rounds of the other's customers sufficiently to keep them quiet and satisfied. Although they were different as night and day in character, they were firm, loving and loyal friends and considered covering one another a part of their duty in life. A friend was a friend and that was that, Mrs. Harris's flat was at No. 5, Willis Gardens, Mrs. Butterfield lived in No. 7, and rare was the day that they did not meet or visit one another to exchange news or confidences.

The taxi crossed a big river, the one Mrs. Harris had seen from the air, now grey instead of blue. On the bridge the driver got himself into a violent argument with another driver. They shouted and screamed at one another. Mrs.

fall back on her friend = be sure that her friend would help her.
make the rounds = visit each in turn.

Harris did not understand the words but guessed at the language and the meaning and smiled happily to herself. This time her thoughts returned to Miss Pamela Penrose and the fuss she had made when informed of Mrs. Harris's intention to take a day off. Mrs. Harris had made it a special point with Mrs. Butterfield to see that the aspiring actress was not neglected.

Curiously, in spite of all her shrewdness and judgement of character Mrs. Harris's favourite of all her clients was Miss Penrose.

The girl, whose real name, as Mrs. Harris had learned from seeing letters that occasionally came so addressed, was Enid Snite, lived untidily in a small flat.

She was a small, smooth good-looking blonde with a tight mouth and eyes that seemed fixed greedily upon but one thing – herself. There was nothing she would not do to advance her career which up to that time had included a year or two in the chorus, some small parts in a few pictures and several appearances on television. She was mean, hard, selfish and merciless, and her manners were hateful as well.

One would have thought that Mrs. Harris would have penetrated the false front of this little beast and abandoned her, for when something about a client displeased Mrs. Harris she simply dropped the key through the letter box and did not return. Like so many of her sisters who did not char for charring's sake alone, even though it was her living, she also brought a certain warmth to it. She had to like either the person or the person's home where she worked.

But it was just the fact that Mrs. Harris had penetrated the front of Miss Snite to a certain extent that made her stick to her, for she understood the fierce, wild, hungry craving of the girl to be something, to be somebody, to lift herself out of the dull ordinariness of everyday struggle and acquire some of the good things of life for herself.

Before her own extraordinary craving which had brought her to Paris Mrs. Harris had not experienced this in herself though she understood it very well. With her it had not been so much the endeavour to make something of herself as a battle to stay alive and in that sense the two of them were not unalike. When Mrs. Harris's husband had died some twenty years ago and left her penniless she simply had to make a go of things, her widow's pension being insufficient.

And then too there was the magic of the theatre which surrounded Miss Snite, or rather Penrose, as Mrs. Harris chose to think of her, and this was irresistible.

Mrs. Harris was not impressed by titles, wealth, position, or family, but she was impressed by the enchantment that enveloped anything or anyone that had to do with the stage, the television, or the pictures.

She had no way of knowing how slender and indefinite was Miss Penrose's connection with these, that she was not only a bad little girl but a not very good actress. It was sufficient for Mrs. Harris that from time to time her voice was heard on the radio or she would pass across the television screen wearing an apron and carrying a tray. Mrs. Harris respected the lone battle the girl was fighting, humoured her, spoiled her and took from her what she would not from anyone else.

make a success of life.
i.e. accepted bad treatment from Miss Penrose which she would not accept from anyone else.

9

The taxi entered a broad street, lined with beautiful buildings, but Mrs. Harris had no eye or time for buildings. She settled back to endure the ride until she should reach the so long desired destination. She reflected upon the strange series of events that led to her being there.

Chapter 2

It had all begun that day several years back when, during the course of her duties at Lady Dant's house, Mrs. Harris had opened a wardrobe to tidy it and had discovered the two dresses hanging there. One was a bit of heaven in cream, ivory, lace and chiffon, the other an explosion in crimson satin with great red bows and a huge red flower. She stood there as though struck dumb, for never in all her life had she seen anything quite as thrilling and beautiful.

Dull and colourless as her existence would seem to have been Mrs. Harris had always felt a craving for beauty and colour which up to this moment had shown itself in a love for flowers. She had both good luck and skill, and plants grew for her where they would not, quite possibly, for any other.

Outside the windows of her flat were two window boxes of geraniums, her favourite flower, and inside, wherever there was room stood a little pot containing a geranium or some other flowering plant bought for a hard-earned five-pence. Then too, the people for whom she worked would sometimes present her with the leavings of their cut flowers which in their fading state she would take home and try to nurse back to health.

As long as she had flowers, Mrs. Harris had no serious complaints concerning the life she led. They were her escape from the gloomy stone desert in which she lived. These bright flashes of colour satisfied her. They were some-

11

thing to return to in the evening, something to wake up to in the morning.

But now as she stood before the wonderful creations hanging in the wardrobe she found herself face to face with a new kind of beauty – an artificial one created by the hand of man the artist, but aimed directly and cunningly at the heart of woman. In that very instant she fell victim to the artist; at that very moment there was born within her the craving to possess such a garment.

There was no rhyme or reason for it, she would never wear such a creation, there was no place in her life for one. Her feeling was purely feminine. She saw it and she wanted it dreadfully. Something inside her craved and reached for it as instinctively as a baby reaches at a bright object. How deeply this craving went, how powerful it was Mrs. Harris herself did not even know at that moment. She could only stand there lost and enchanted, gazing at the dresses, leaning upon her mop, in her working shoes, and work-stained apron, her hair down about her ears, the traditional figure of the cleaning woman.

It was thus that Lady Dant found her when she happened to come in from her writing-room. 'Oh!' she exclaimed, 'my dresses!' And then noting Mrs. Harris's attitude and the expression on her face said: 'Do you like them?'

Mrs. Harris was hardly conscious that Lady Dant was speaking, she was still so lost in these living creations of silks and chiffons in heart-lifting colours, daring design and stiff with cunning internal construction so that they

creation = something that is made, and, especially, a very expensive lady's dress.
rhyme or reason = sense or meaning.

appeared to stand almost by themselves like creatures with a life of their own. 'Coo,' she gasped finally, 'aren't they beauties. They must have cost a fortune.'

Lady Dant laughed her dry laugh and said: 'Well, yes, in a way. This one here cost three hundred and fifty pounds and the big one, the red, came to around four hundred and fifty. I always go to Dior. Then, of course, you know you're right. Don't you agree?'

'Four hundred and fifty pounds,' echoed Mrs. Harris. 'How would anyone ever get that much money?' She was not unfamiliar with Paris styles, for she was an eager reader of old fashion magazines sometimes presented to her by clients, and she had heard of Dior.

But it was one thing to encounter photographs of dresses, looking through the smart pages of *Vogue* or *Elle* where, whether in colour or black and white, they were impersonal and as out of her world and her reach as the moon or the stars. It was quite another to come face to face with the real article, to feast one's eyes upon its every clever stitch, to touch it, smell it, love it, and suddenly to become burned up with the fires of desire.

Mrs. Harris was quite unaware that in her reply to Lady Dant she had already given voice to a determination to possess a dress such as this. She had not meant 'how would anyone find that much money?' but 'how would *I* find that much money?' There was, of course, no answer to this, or rather only one. One would have to win it. But the chances of this were likewise as remote as the planets.

Lady Dant was quite well pleased with the impression she seemed to have created and even took each one down

---

Vogue and *Elle* are two magazines devoted to expensive ladies' clothes.

and held it up to her so that Mrs. Harris could get some idea of the effect. And since the char's hands were spotless from the soap and water in which they were dipped most of the time, she let her touch the materials.

'Aren't they beauties?' she whispered again. Lady Dant did not know that at that instant Mrs. Harris had made up her mind that what she desired above all else on earth, and in Heaven thereafter, was to have a Dior dress of her own hanging in her cupboard.

Smiling, pleased with herself, Lady Dant shut the wardrobe door, but she could not shut out from the mind of Mrs. Harris what she had seen there: beauty, perfection, the ultimate in adornment that a woman could desire. Mrs. Harris was no less a woman than Lady Dant or any other. She wanted, she wanted, she wanted a dress from what must surely be the most expensive shop in the world, that of Mr. Dior in Paris.

Mrs. Harris was no fool. Not so much as a thought of ever wearing such a garment in public ever entered her head. But it was possession she desired now, feminine physical possession: to have it hanging in her cupboard, to know that it was there when she was away, to open the door when she returned and find it waiting for her, exquisite to touch, to see and to own. It was as though all she had missed in life through the poverty, the circumstances of her birth and class in life could be made up by becoming the holder of this one glorious bit of feminine finery. The same vast, unthinkable amount of money could be represented as well by a piece of jewellery, or a single diamond which would last for ever. Mrs. Harris had no interest in diamonds. The very fact that one dress could represent such a huge sum increased its desirability and her yearning for it. She was well aware that her wanting it made no sense at all, but that did not prevent her from doing so.

All through the rest of that damp, miserable and foggy day, she was warmed by the images of the creations she had seen, and the more she thought of them the more the craving grew upon her.

That evening as the rain dripped from the thick London fog, Mrs. Harris sat in the friendly warmth of Mrs. Butterfield's kitchen for the important ceremony of making out their coupons for the weekly football pool.

Ever since she could remember, it seemed that she and Mrs. Butterfield had been contributing their four pence a week to this fascinating national gamble. It was cheap at the price, the hope and excitement that could be bought for no more than four pence each. For once the coupon was filled in and dropped into the post box it represented unimaginable wealth until the arrival of the newspapers with the results and disillusionment, but never really disappointment since they actually did not expect to win. Once Mrs. Harris had achieved a prize of one pound fifty pence, but that was all. The fantastic major prizes remained ambition-inspiring fairy tales that occasionally found their way into the newspapers.

Since Mrs. Harris was not sports-minded nor had the time to follow the fortunes of the football teams she was accustomed to making out her selections by guess and by luck.

On this particular evening as they sat in the pool of lamplight, their coupons and steaming cups of tea before them, Mrs. Harris felt the presence of luck as thickly about her as the fog outside. As her pencil hovered over the first line — 'Aston Villa v. Bolton Wanderers' — she looked up

two English football teams.

15

and said to Mrs. Butterfield: 'This is for my Dior dress.'

'Your what, dearie?' asked Mrs. Butterfield.

'My Dior dress,' repeated Mrs. Harris and then said fiercely as though by her very fierceness to force it to happen, 'I'm going to have a Dior dress.'

'Are you now?' murmured Mrs. Butterfield.

'Haven't you ever heard of Dior?' said Mrs. Harris.

'Can't say I have, love,' Mrs. Butterfield replied.

'It's the most expensive shop in the world. It's in Paris. The dresses cost four hundred and fifty pounds.'

'Four hundred and fifty what?' gasped Mrs. Butterfield, 'have you gone mad, dearie?'

For a moment even Mrs. Harris was shocked by the figure, but then its very outrageousness, together with the force of the desire that had been born within her, restored her conviction. She said: 'Lady Dant has one of them in her cupboard. I've never seen anything like it in my life before except perhaps in a dream or in a book.' Her voice lowered for a moment as she became reflective. 'Why even the Queen hasn't got a dress like that,' she said, and then loudly and firmly, 'and I mean to have one.'

The shock waves had now begun to die down in Mrs. Butterfield and she returned to her practical gloominess. 'Where're you going to get the money, dearie?' she asked.

'Right here,' replied Mrs. Harris tapping her coupon with her pencil so as to leave fate in no doubt as to what was expected of it.

Mrs. Butterfield accepted this since she herself had a long list of articles she expected to acquire immediately should *her* coupon ever be lucky. But she had another idea. 'Dresses like that aren't for people like us, dearie,' she gloomed.

Mrs. Harris reacted passionately: 'What do I care what is or isn't for people like us; it's the most beautiful thing I've ever seen and I mean to have it.'

Mrs. Butterfield persisted: 'What would you do with it when you got it?'

This brought Mrs. Harris up short, for she had not even thought beyond the possession of such a wonderful creation. All she knew was that she craved it most fearfully and so to Mrs. Butterfield's question she could make no other reply than: 'Have it! Just have it!'

Her pencil was resting on the first line of the pool coupon. She turned her attention to it and said: 'Now then, off we go!' And without another moment's hesitation, almost as though her fingers were working outside her own will, she filled in line after line, win, lose, draw, win, win, draw, draw, draw, lose and win, until the entire coupon was completed. She had never done it like that before. 'There,' she said.

'Good luck to you, love,' said Mrs. Butterfield.

Still in the grip of something, Mrs. Harris said hoarsely: 'Let's post them now, right now while my luck is running.'

They put on coats, wound scarves about their heads and went off into the rain and the dripping fog to the red post box gleaming faintly on the corner beneath the street-lamp. Mrs. Harris pressed the envelope to her lips for a moment, said 'Here's for my Dior dress,' and slipped the letter into the box, listening for its fall. Mrs. Butterfield posted hers with less confidence. 'Don't expect anything and you won't get disappointed. That's my motto,' she said. They returned to their tea.

This made Mrs. Harris suddenly stop to think.

18

The marvellous and universe-shattering discovery was made that week-end not by Mrs. Harris, but by Mrs. Butterfield, who came storming into the former's kitchen in such a state that she was hardly able to speak.

'D-d-d-dearie –,' she stammered – 'dearie, it's *happened*!' Mrs. Butterfield waved the newspaper – 'You've won!'

The full import of what her friend was saying did not reach Mrs. Harris at once, for having placed her ultimate fate in the hands of the powerful feeling of luck, she had then temporarily put the matter from her mind. But at last the meaning of what Mrs. Butterfield was shouting came to her and she dropped her iron to the floor with a crash. 'My Dior dress!' she cried, and the next moment she had seized her stout friend about the waist and the two of them were dancing like children about the kitchen.

Then, lest there be a mistake they had to sit down, and carefully, score by score, figure by figure (for, of course, they kept copies of their selections), check the results of that Saturday's contests. It was true. But for two games, Mrs. Harris had made a perfect score. There would be a prize, a rich one, certainly, perhaps even the top prize, depending upon whether anyone else had surpassed or matched Mrs. Harris's effort.

One thing seemed certain, however, the Dior dress, or at least the money for it was assured, for neither could conceive that the prize for achieving twelve out of fourteen games could be less. But there was one great trial yet to be undergone by both. They would have to wait until Wednesday before being advised by telegram of the amount of Mrs. Harris's winnings.

'Whatever's over from what I need for my dress, I'll split with you,' the little charwoman told her stout friend in a moment of warm generosity and meant every word of it. In the first flush of excitement over the win Mrs. Harris saw herself marching through this Dior's shop attended by bowing sales staff. Her handbag would be filled to bursting with the stuff. She would walk down aisle after aisle, past rack after rack of wondrous garments standing stiff with satin, lace and velvets to make her choice finally and say – 'I'll have *that* one.'

And yet – and yet – Mrs. Harris could not help harbouring a suspicion gathered from the task of the living of daily life and making a go of things that it might not be very easy. To crave something exquisite but useless, a luxury wholly out of one's reach, to pin one's faith in getting it on a gamble and to draw immediately the winning number, this was story-book stuff.

Still, it did seem to happen to people from time to time. One kept reading of such events in the newspapers every other day. Well, there was nothing to do but wait until Wednesday. But there was no disputing the facts and figures, or that she was a winner, for she had checked them over time and time again. The Dior dress would be hers, and perhaps much, much more even when she split with

stuff – here used as slang for ' money '.
making things go right, making a success.
The sort of thing one reads in story books.

Mrs. Butterfield. A top pool had been known to yield as much as a hundred and fifty thousand pounds. Thus she wavered for three days until Wednesday morning when the fateful telegram from the pool headquarters arrived. It was the measure of her affection for her friend that she did not tear it open at once to learn its contents, but held back until she was fully dressed and could run over to Mrs. Butterfield, who braced herself in a chair for the big moment, fanning herself with her apron, crying: 'For the Lord's sake, love, open it or I'll die of excitement.'

At last, with trembling fingers, Mrs. Harris opened the envelope and unfolded the message. It advised her briefly that her coupon had been a winning one and that her share would be one hundred and two pounds forty-eight pence. It was well in a way that Mrs. Harris had entertained the possibility of a let-down, for the sum was so much less than what she needed to become the possessor of a dress from Dior that the realisation of her dream was as far away and seemingly impossible as ever. Not even Mrs. Butterfield's comforting – 'Well, it's better than nothing; a lot of folks would be glad of the money' could help her to overcome her initial disappointment, even though she knew in her heart of hearts that that was what life was like.

What had happened? A list of winners sent to Mrs. Harris a few days later made it plain enough. It had been a hard week in the football league with many upsets. While no one had picked all fourteen games correctly or even thirteen, a considerable number had equalled Mrs. Harris's effort, shrinking the share for each one.

One hundred and two pounds forty-eight pence was a sum not to be despised and yet for several days it left

deep inside her.

Mrs. Harris with rather a dull feeling about the heart and at night she would awaken with a feeling of sadness and unshed tears and then she would remember why.

Once the disappointment was over, Mrs. Harris would have thought that the excitement of winning a hundred pounds in the football pool – a hundred pounds to be spent upon anything she liked – would have put an end to her desire for the Dior dress. Yet the contrary proved to be the case. Her yearning was as strong as ever. She could not put it out of her mind. In the morning when she woke up, it was to a feeling of sadness and emptiness as though something unpleasant had happened to her, or something was missing which sleep had temporarily obscured. Then she would realise that it was the Dior dress, or *a* Dior dress – just one, once in her lifetime that she was still craving and would never have.

And at night, when after her final cup of tea and chat with Mrs. Butterfield she joined her old friends the hot water bottles in her bed and pulled the sheets up about her chin, there would begin a desperate struggle to think of something else.

But it was no use. The more she tried to think of other things the more the Dior dress intruded into her consciousness, and she lay there in the darkness, shivering and craving for it. Even with the light out and no more than the gleam of the street lamp shining into the bedroom window, she could look right through the cupboard door and imagine it hanging there. The colour and the materials kept changing, sometimes she saw it in pink or crimson satin, at other times in white with ivory laces. But always it was the most beautiful and expensive thing of its kind. The desire to possess such a thing was immovably fixed in her mind. Sometimes the longing was so strong that it would bring tears to her eyes before she fell asleep, and often it continued in some strange dream.

But one night, a week or so later, Mrs. Harris's thoughts took a new direction. She reflected upon the evening she had made out the football coupon with Mrs. Butterfield and the curious sense of certainty she had experienced that this would win her the coveted dress. The results, it is true, had been in line with what she knew by experience. They were the disappointments of life, and yet after all, were they? She had won a hundred pounds, no, more, a hundred and two pounds forty-eight pence.

Why then this curious sum, what the message or the meaning it held for her? For Mrs. Harris's world was filled with signals, signs and messages from On High. With the price of a Dior dress of four hundred and fifty pounds, three hundred and fifty pounds was still wholly out of her reach. But wait! A flash of understanding and inspiration came to her and she snapped on the light and sat up in bed with the sheer excitement of it. It was not really three hundred and fifty pounds any longer. She had not only her hundred pounds in the bank, but a start of two pounds forty-eight pence on the second hundred, and once she had achieved that, the third hundred pounds would no longer be so difficult.

'That's it,' said Mrs. Harris to herself aloud. 'I'll have it if it's the last thing I do and it takes the rest of my life.' She got out of bed secured pencil and paper and began to work it out.

Mrs. Harris had never in her life paid more than five pounds for a dress, a sum she noted down on the paper

from On High = from heaven.

23

opposite the utterly fantastic figure of four hundred and fifty pounds. Had Lady Dant named some such sum as fifty or sixty pounds as the price of the marvellous creations in her wardrobe it is quite possible that Mrs. Harris would have put the entire matter out of her head immediately as not only a gap in price she was not prepared to consider, but also a matter of class upon which she preferred not to venture.

But the very outrageousness of the sum made it all a wholly different matter. What is it that makes a woman yearn for a Rolls-Royce or jewels from Cartier, or the most expensive perfume, restaurant, or neighbourhood to live in? It is this very peak and outrageousness of price that is the guarantee of the value of her own femininity and person. Mrs. Harris simply felt that if one owned a dress so beautiful that it cost four hundred and fifty pounds, then there was nothing left upon earth to be desired. Her pencil began to move across the paper.

She earned fifteen pence an hour. She worked ten hours a day, six days a week, fifty-two weeks in the year. Mrs. Harris screwed her tongue into her cheek and applied the multiplication table, reaching the figure of four hundred and sixty-eight pounds per annum, just the price of one of the more expensive Dior dresses plus the amount of the fare to Paris and back.

Now, with equal determination Mrs. Harris began a second column, rent, taxes, food, medicine, shoes, and all the little expenses of living of which she could think. The task was a staggering one when she took away expenses from income. Years of saving lay ahead of her, two at the very least, if not three unless she had some other stroke of luck or a shower of tips. But the figures shook neither her confidence nor her determination. On the contrary they strengthened them. 'I'll have it,' she said once more and turned out the light. She went to sleep immediately, peacefully as a child, and when she awoke the following morning she felt no longer sad but only eager and excited as one who is about to set out upon a great and unknown adventure.

The matter came out into the open next evening, their regular night to go to the cinema, when Mrs. Butterfield appeared as usual shortly after eight, wrapped against the cold and was surprised to find Mrs. Harris in her kitchen unprepared for any expedition, and examining newspaper advertisements headed – 'EARN MONEY IN YOUR LEISURE TIME AT HOME.'

'We'll be late, dearie,' warned Mrs. Butterfield.

Mrs. Harris looked at her friend guiltily. 'I'm not going,' she said.

'Not going to the pictures?' echoed the astounded Mrs. Butterfield. 'But it's Marilyn Monroe.'

'I can't help it. I can't go. I'm saving my money.'

'Lord bless us,' said Mrs. Butterfield. 'Whatever for?'

Mrs. Harris breathed deeply before she replied: 'My Dior dress.'

'Lord love you, dearie, you *have* gone mad. I thought you said the dress cost four hundred and fifty pounds.'

I've already got a hundred and two pounds forty-eight pence,' Mrs. Harris said. 'I'm saving up for the rest.'

Mrs. Butterfield's chins quivered as she shook her head in admiration. 'Character, that's what you've got,' she said. 'I never could do it myself. Tell you what, dear, you come along with me. I'll treat you.'

But Mrs. Harris was quite firm, 'I can't,' she said. 'I

wouldn't be able to treat you back.'

Mrs. Butterfield sighed a heavy sigh and began to take off her outer clothing. 'Oh, well,' she said, 'I guess Marilyn Monroe isn't everything. I'd just as soon have a cup of tea and a quiet chat.'

Mrs. Harris accepted the sacrifice her friend was making, but her glance travelled guiltily to the tea tin. It was full enough now, but soon would be inhospitably empty. For this was one of the things on her list to cut down. She put the kettle on.

Thus began a long, hard period of saving and doing without, none of which in the least interfered with Mrs. Harris's good humour with the exception that she denied herself the occasional pot of flowers in season and more than ever watched over the health of her beloved geraniums lest she be unable to replace them.

She went without cigarettes – and a quiet smoke used to be a comfort – and without gin. She walked instead of taking the bus or the underground and when holes appeared in her shoes she padded them with newspaper. She gave up her cherished evening papers and got her news and gossip a day late out of the waste-paper baskets of her clients. She saved on food and clothing. The former might have been injurious, except that Mrs. Schreiber, the American woman, where she was usually working around lunch time, was generous and always offered her an egg or something cold from the refrigerator. This she now accepted.

But the cinema saw her no more, nor did The Crown, the pub on the corner; she went, herself, almost tea-less so that there might be some in the tin when it was Mrs. Butterfield's turn to visit her. And she came near to ruining her eyes with some badly paid home-work which she did at night, sewing zips on to the backs of cheap dresses. The only thing Mrs. Harris did not give up was the four pence a week for the football pool, but, of course, lightning had no intention whatever of striking twice in this same place. Nevertheless she felt she could not afford not to continue paying it.

Through discarded six months old fashion magazines she kept up with the doings of Christian Dior, and always before her eyes, buoying her up and stiffening her backbone was the knowledge that one of these days, in the not too distant future, one of these wonderful creations would be hers.

And while Mrs. Butterfield did not change her opinion that no good could come from wanting things above one's station and somewhere along the line Mrs. Harris would encounter disaster, she nevertheless admired her friend's determination and courage and stoutly supported her, helping her wherever she could, and, of course, keeping her secret, for Mrs. Harris told no one else of her plans and ambitions.

Lightning never strikes in the same place twice ' is a saying meaning that a piece of luck does not repeat itself.
    above one's social class.
    somewhere in the course of her plan.

Chapter 4

Somehow the little charwoman had come across two important bits of information. There were currency restrictions which forbade exporting more than ten pounds out of Great Britain and therefore no French shop would accept a large sum of money in pounds, but demanded another currency. So it would have done her no good to have smuggled out such a sum as four hundred and fifty pounds, nor would she have done so.

For Mrs. Harris's moral code was both strict and practical. She would tell a fib but not a lie. She would not break the law, but she was not unwilling to bend it as far as it would go. She was completely honest but at the same time was not to be considered a fool.

Since pounds were forbidden as well as useless in quantities in Paris, she needed some other medium of exchange and hit upon dollars. And for dollars there was one person to whom she could turn, the friendly, kind and not-too-bright American lady, Mrs. Schreiber.

Mrs. Harris conveniently invented a nephew in America who was apparently very much in need and to whom she was compelled to send money.

Mrs. Schreiber, who was more than a bit vague herself with regard to British currency laws, saw no reason why she should not aid such a good-hearted person as Mrs. Harris, and since she was wealthy and possessed an almost

thought of the idea of.

limitless supply of dollars, or could get fresh ones whenever she wanted them, Mrs. Harris's slowly growing pile of pounds got themselves translated into American currency. It became an accepted thing week by week this exchange. Mrs. Schreiber likewise paid her in dollars and tipped her in dollars and nobody was any the wiser.

Slowly but surely over a period of two years the bundle of five, ten and twenty dollar bills grew in size until one fresh morning, early in January, counting her hoard and thumbing her bank book, Mrs. Harris knew that she was no longer too far away from the realisation of her dream.

It was on a May morning, four months later, or to be exact two years, seven months, three weeks and one day following her resolve to own a Dior dress, that Mrs. Harris, firm and fully equipped beneath the green hat with the pink rose was seen off on the bus to the Air Station by a trembling and nervous Mrs. Butterfield. Besides the slowly and carefully saved fortune, the price of the dress, she was equipped with passport, return ticket to Paris and sufficient funds to get there and back.

The intended schedule of her day included the selection and purchase of her dress, lunch in Paris, a bit of sightseeing and return by the evening plane.

The clients had all been warned of the unusual event of Mrs. Harris's taking a day off, with Mrs. Butterfield substituting, and had reacted in accordance with their characters and natures. It was the actress, Miss Pamela Penrose, who kicked up the ugliest fuss, storming at the little char. 'But that's horrid of you. You can't. I won't hear of it. I pay you, don't I? I've got a most important producer coming for drinks here tomorrow. You charwomen are all alike.

nobody else knew anything about it.

29

Never think of anybody but yourselves. I do think, after all I've done for you, you might show me a little consideration.'

For a moment, Mrs. Harris was tempted to reveal where she was off to and why – and resisted. The love affair between herself and the Dior dress was private. Instead she said soothingly: 'Now, now, love, no need for you to get angry. My friend, Mrs. Butterfield, will look in on you on her way home tomorrow and give the place a good tidying up. Your producer friend won't know the difference. Well, dearie, here's hoping he gives you a good job,' she concluded cheerily and left Miss Penrose frowning and bad-tempered.

Chapter 5

All thoughts of the actress, and for that matter all of her wandering back into the past, were driven out of Mrs. Harris's head when with a jerk and a scream of brakes the cab came to a halt at what must be her destination.

The great grey building that is the House of Christian Dior occupies an entire corner of the Avenue Montaigne. It has two entrances, one which leads through the Boutique where small articles are sold at prices ranging from five to a hundred pounds, and another more exclusive one.

The cab driver chose to leave Mrs. Harris at the latter, reserved for the genuinely rich clients, assuming his passenger to be at the very least an English noblewoman. Then crying to her gaily the only English he knew, which was 'How do you do,' he drove off leaving her standing on the sidewalk before the place that had occupied her yearnings and dreams and ambitions for the past three years.

And a strange uncertainty stirred in the thin breast beneath the brown coat. It was no store at all like Selfridge's in Oxford Street, or Marks & Spencer, where she did her shopping, not a proper store at all, with windows for display and wax figures with pearly smiles and pink cheeks, arms outstretched in elegant attitudes to show off the clothes that were for sale. There was nothing, nothing at all, but some windows shaded by grey curtains, and a

popular, well known shops in London.
smiles showing teeth as white as pearls.

31

door. True, above the arch of the entrance were cut the words 'CHRISTIAN DIOR', but no other identification.

Standing alone now in a foreign city, assailed by the foreign roar of foreign traffic and the foreign bustle of foreign passers-by, outside the great, grey building that was like a private house and not a shop at all, Mrs. Harris suddenly felt lonely, frightened and forlorn, and in spite of the great roll of silver-green American dollars in her handbag she wished for a moment that she had not come, or that she had asked the young man from the Airlines to accompany her, or that the taxi driver had not driven away leaving her standing there.

And then, as luck would have it, a car from the British Embassy drove by and the sight of the tiny Union Jack flying from it stiffened her spine and brought determination to her mouth and eyes. She reminded herself who and what she was, drew in a deep breath of the Paris air and pushed open the door and entered.

She was almost driven back by the powerful smell of elegance that assailed her once she was inside. It was the same that she smelled when Lady Dant opened the doors to her wardrobe, the one she sometimes sniffed in the streets when, as she passed, someone opened the door of a luxurious motor car. It was compounded of perfume and fur and satins, silks and leather, jewellery and face powder. It seemed to arise from the thick grey carpets and hangings, and fill the air of the grand staircase before her.

It was the odour of the rich, and it made her tremble once more and wonder what she, Ada Harris, was doing there instead of washing up the luncheon dishes for Mrs. Fford Foulks at home, or advancing the career of a real theatrical star like Pamela Penrose by seeing that her flat

32

was neat and tidy when her producer friends came to call.

She hesitated, her feet seemingly sinking into the thick carpet up to her ankles. Then her fingers crept into her handbag and tested the smooth feel of the roll of American bills. 'That's why you're here, Ada Harris. That says you're as rich as any of them. Get on with it then, my girl.'

She mounted the imposing and deserted staircase, it then being half-past eleven in the morning. On the first landing there was but a single silver slipper in a glass showcase set into the wall, on the second turn there was a similar show-case housing a huge bottle of Dior perfume. But otherwise there were no goods of any kind on display, nor were there crowds of people rushing up and down the stairs as in Marks & Spencer's or Selfridge's. Nowhere was there any sign of anything that looked like the shops to which she was accustomed.

On the contrary, the elegance and atmosphere of the deserted staircase gave her the feeling of a private house, and one on a most grand scale at that. Was she really in the right place? Her courage threatened to disappear again, but she told herself that sooner or later she must come upon some human being who would be able to direct her to the dresses, or at least put her right if she were in the wrong building. She pressed on and indeed on the first-floor landing came upon a dark handsome woman in her early forties who was writing at a desk. She wore a simple black dress relieved by three rows of pearls at the neck, her hair was neat and shining; her features were refined, her skin exquisite, but closer inspection would have revealed that

at that = moreover.

she looked tired and care-worn and that there were dark hollows beneath her eyes.

Behind her, Mrs. Harris noted a fair-sized room opening into a second one, grey-carpeted like the stairs, with fine silk hangings at the windows, and furnished only with several rows of grey and golden chairs around the walls and a few floor-to-ceiling mirrors. Of anything to sell or even so much as to look at, there was not a sign.

Mme Colbert, the manageress, had had a bad morning. A usually kind and gracious lady, she had let herself quarrel with M. Fauvel, the young and handsome head of the accounts department, of whom otherwise she was rather fond, and had sent him upstairs again to his office with his ears reddening.

It was merely a matter of his enquiring about a client whose bills seemed to run too long without payment. On any other day Mme Colbert might have favoured the accountant with a humorous summing-up of the client's characteristics and honesty. Instead of which she complained angrily to him that it was her business to sell dresses and his to collect the money and she had not the time to inspect the bank accounts of clients. That was his affair.

Besides giving short answers all morning, she had scolded several of the sales-girls and even permitted herself to scold Natasha, the star model of the House, for being late for a fitting, when, as she knew well, the Metro and the buses were engaging in a go-slow strike. What made it worse was that the exquisite Natasha had replied to the sharp words in a most un-starlike manner, she did not argue or snap back, only two large tears formed at her eyes and rolled down her cheeks.

And then besides, Mme Colbert was not at all sure that she had not made a mistake with the invitations and seating for the afternoon's review of the collection. As head of the department she was an important and all-powerful person on the first floor. It was she who issued or denied invitations to see the collection. She was in charge of seating arrangements, and clients must be placed according to importance, rank, title and bank-roll.

When such a powerful person was unwell or ill-humoured, the results were felt far and wide. The trouble which Mme Colbert was suffering had to do with her husband Jules and the love, respect and affection for him which had grown over the twenty years they had been together. Dear, good, decent, clever Jules, who had more knowledge in one finger-tip than all the rest of them in the Foreign Office, with their rosettes and political connections. But one thing Jules lacked, or rather two – he had not the ability to push himself and – he had no political friends or connections.

Beginning as a poor boy he had achieved his position by brilliance and application. Yet, whenever there was a better or higher position opening he was rejected in favour of someone of lesser intelligence but greater connections. Mme Colbert knew that many a difficult problem had been solved by her husband's brains. Yet, time and time again he had been refused a higher post, time and time again his eagerness had been shattered. In the past year for the first time Mme Colbert had become aware of a growing hopelessness in her husband. Now a man of fifty he felt he could

collection of dresses.
a small imitation rose worn by a Frenchman to whom a high honour (membership of the Légion d'Honneur) has been given.
application = hard work.

look forward to nothing better. He had almost given up and it broke her heart to see the changes in the man to whom she had given her devotion.

Recently, the chief of an important department in the Foreign Office had died. Speculation was plentiful as to who would replace him. Jules Colbert was one of those in line for the job and yet –

It saddened Mme Colbert almost to the point of desperation to see how her husband's buoyancy from his younger days struggled to break through the weight of hopelessness that experience had laid upon his shoulders. He dared to hope again, even against all of the political corruption which would shatter his hopes and this time leave him an old and broken man.

This then was the burden that Mme Colbert carried about with her. She loved her husband and could not bear to see him destroyed, but neither could she do anything to prevent it and break the ugly pattern of his being pushed aside in favour of someone who had the right connections of money, family, or political power. She lay awake at nights searching her brains for some means to help him. By day she could only become more and more convinced of the uselessness of her efforts, and thus her bitterness was carried on into the life of her daily work and began to affect those about her. She was not unaware of the change in herself: she seemed to be going about in some kind of frightening dream from which she could not awake.

Seated now at her desk on the first-floor landing and trying to concentrate on the placing of the guests for the afternoon show, Mme Colbert looked up to see a figure ascending the stairs which caused a shudder to pass through her frame and led her to brush her hand across her brow and eyes as though to clear away an imagined ghost, if it was one. But it was not. She was real enough.

One of Mme Colbert's skills was her unvarying judgment in estimating the quality of would-be customers or clients, distinguishing the genuine ones from the time-wasters, penetrating outward appearances to the bankrolls within. But this woman ascending the stairs in the worn, shabby coat, gloves of the wrong colour, shoes that advertised only too plainly her origin, the dreadful imitation-leather handbag, and the wholly absurd hat with its huge pink rose, defied her.

If the creature had been what she looked like, a cleaning woman (and here you see how marvellous Mme Colbert's instincts were), she would have been entering by the back way. But, of course, this was absurd since all of the cleaning was done there at night, after hours. It was impossible that this could be a client of or for the House of Dior.

And yet she waited for the woman to speak, for she realised that she was so upset by her own personal problems that her judgment might be faulty. She had not long to wait.

'Ah, there you are, dearie,' the woman said, 'could you tell me which way to the dresses?'

Madame Colbert no longer had any doubts as to her judgment. Such a voice and such an accent had not been heard inside the walls of the House of Dior since its foundation.

'The dresses?' enquired Mme Colbert in chilled and faultless English, 'what dresses?'

'Oh come now, dearie,' encouraged Mrs. Harris, 'aren't you a bit slow this morning? Where is it they hang up the dresses for sale?'

For one moment Mme Colbert thought that this strange person might have strayed from looking for the little shop below. 'If you mean the Boutique —'

Mrs. Harris frowned. 'Bou – what? I didn't ask for any booties. It's the dresses I want, the expensive ones. Pull yourself together, dearie, I've come all the way from London to buy myself one of your dresses and I haven't any time to waste.'

All was as clear as day to Mme Colbert now. Occasionally an error came marching up the grand staircase, though never before one quite so obvious and dreadful as this one, and had to be dealt with firmly. Her own troubles rendered the manageress colder and more unsympathetic than usual in such circumstances. 'I am afraid you have come to the wrong place. We do not display dresses here. The collection is only shown privately in the afternoons.'

Mrs. Harris was completely bewildered. 'What collection? I don't want any collection. Is this Dior or isn't it?' Then, before the woman could reply she remembered something. She used to encounter the word 'collections' in the fashion magazines. Now her natural shrewdness cut through the mystery. 'Look here,' she said, 'maybe it *is* this collection I want to see, what about it?'

Impatience seized Mme Colbert, who was anxious to return to the miseries of her own thoughts. 'I am sorry,' she said coldly, 'the salon is filled for this afternoon and the rest of the week.' To get rid of her finally she repeated the usual formula: 'If you will leave the name of your hotel, perhaps next week some time we can send you an invitation.'

Righteous anger filled the bosom of Mrs. Harris. She

make an effort.

moved a step nearer to Mme Colbert and the pink rose attached to the front of the hat waved wildly as she cried with deep bitterness: 'Oh that's a good one. You'll send me an invitation to spend my money hard-earned dusting and mopping and running my hands in dirty dish water, next week, *per*haps – me that's got to be back in London tonight. How do you like that?'

The rose waved menacingly a foot from Mme Colbert's face. 'See here, Miss Smooth-Talk, if you don't think I've got the money to pay for what I want – *here*!' And with this Mrs. Harris opened the imitation leather bag and turned it upside down. The rubber band about her roll chose that moment to burst, dramatically showering a green flood of American five, ten, and twenty dollar notes. 'There!' at which point Mrs. Harris raised her voice to roof level, 'what's the matter with that? Isn't my money as good as anybody else's?'

Caught by surprise Mme Colbert stared at the astonishing and, truth to tell, beautiful sight, murmuring to herself 'Mon Dieu! better than most people's.' Her mind had turned suddenly to her recent quarrel with young André Fauvel who had complained about clients not paying their bills. There was no denying that the mound of dollars on the desk was real money.

But Mme Colbert was now confused as well as surprised by the appearance and manner of this strange customer. How had she, who professed to scrub floors and wash dishes for her living, come by so much money and in dollars at that? And what on earth did she want with a Dior dress? The whole business indicated irregularity leading to trouble. Nowhere did it add up or make sense, and Mme Colbert

come by = obtain.

felt she had enough trouble as it was without becoming involved with this impossible British visitor who had more money on her person than she ought.

Quite firmly, in spite of the sea of green dollars covering her desk, Mme Colbert repeated: 'I am sorry, the salon is full this afternoon.'

Mrs. Harris's lips began to tremble and her little eyes screwed up as the real meaning of the disaster became clear. Here, in this apparently empty, hostile building, before cold, hostile eyes, the unimaginable seemed about to happen. They didn't seem to want her, they didn't even appear to want her money. They were going to send her away and back to London without her Dior dress.

'Oh!' she cried, 'haven't you French people got any heart? You there, so smooth and cool! Didn't you ever want anything so bad you could cry every time you thought about it? Haven't you ever stayed awake at nights wanting something and shivering, because maybe you couldn't ever have it?'

Her words struck like a knife to the heart of Mme Colbert who night after night had been doing just that, lying awake and shivering from the ache to be able to do something for her man. And the pain of the thrust forced a little cry from the manageress. 'How did you know? How ever could you guess?'

Her own dark unhappy eyes suddenly became caught up in the small vivid blue ones of Mrs. Harris which were revealing the first sign of tears. Woman looked into woman, and what Mme Colbert saw filled her first with horror and then a sudden rush of compassion and understanding.

The horror was directed at herself, at her own coldness

so bad = so very much.

and lack of sympathy. In one moment it seemed this odd little woman facing her had held a mirror up and let her see herself as she had become through self-indulgence and yielding to her personal difficulties. She thought with shame how she had behaved towards M. Fauvel, the sales girls and even Natasha, the model.

But above all she was appalled at the realisation that she had let herself be so hardened by the thoughts with which she lived daily that she had become both blind and deaf to human needs and cries arising from the human heart. Wherever she came from, whatever her walk in life, the person opposite her was a woman, with all of a woman's desires, and as the blindness fell thus from her own eyes, she whispered: 'My dear, you've set your heart on a Dior dress.'

Mme Colbert was looking now at the pile of money and shaking her head in amazement. 'But however did you – ?'

'Did without things and saved,' said Mrs. Harris. 'It's taken me three years. But if you want something bad enough, there are always ways. Mind you, you've got to have a bit of luck as well. Now take me, after I won a hundred pounds on a football pool I said to myself, "That's a sign, Ada Harris," so I started saving and here I am.'

Mme Colbert realised what 'Saving' meant to such a person and a wave of admiration for the courage and gallantry of the woman passed through her. Perhaps if she herself had shown more of this kind of courage and determination, she might have been able to accomplish something for her husband. She passed her hand over her brow again and came to a quick decision. 'What is your name,

social position.
take me as an example.

my dear?' When Mrs. Harris told her she filled it in quickly on a printed card that said that Monsieur Christian Dior would be honoured by her presence at the showing of his collection that afternoon. 'Come back at three,' she said and handed it to Mrs. Harris. 'There really *is* no room, but I will make a place for you on the stairs from where you will be able to see the collection.'

All anger and sadness vanished from the voice of Mrs. Harris as she gazed in ecstasy at her admission to Paradise. 'Now that's kind of you, love,' she said. 'It looks as if my luck is holding out.'

A curious feeling of peace filled Mme Colbert and a strange smile illuminated her countenance as she said: 'Who can say, perhaps you will be lucky for me too.'

Chapter 6

At five minutes to three that afternoon three people, whose lives were to become strangely joined together, found themselves within a whisper of one another by the grand staircase in the House of Dior, now crowded with visitors, clients, sales girls, staff and members of the press.

The first of these was M. André Fauvel, the chief accountant, a well built, handsome young man. It was sometimes necessary for him to descend from the chilling regions of his account books on the fourth floor to the warmth of the atmosphere of perfumes, silks and satins and the females they clothed on the first floor. He welcomed these occasions and even sought excuses for them in the expectation of catching a glimpse of his goddess, the star model, with whom he was desperately and, of course, quite hopelessly in love.

For Mlle Natasha, as she was known to press and public in the fashion world, was the favourite of Paris, a dark-haired, dark-eyed beauty of extraordinary attraction and one who surely had a brilliant career before her either in films or a rich and titled marriage. Every important bachelor in Paris was paying her attention.

M. Fauvel came from a good middle-class family; his was a good position with a good wage, and he had a little money besides, but his world was as far removed from the brilliant star of Natasha as was the planet earth from the great Sirius.

He was fortunate, for that moment he did catch a sight of her in the doorway of the dressing-room, already wearing the first dress she was to model. M. Fauvel thought that his heart would stop and never beat again, so beautiful was she and so unattainable.

Glancing out of her sweet, grave eyes, Mlle Natasha saw M. Fauvel and yet saw him not, as, showing a tip of pink tongue, she stifled a yawn. For, in fact, she was very, very tired and uninterested. None but a few at Dior's knew the real identity much less the real personality of the long-limbed, high-waisted, black-haired beauty who attracted the rich and famous to her side like flies.

Her real name then was Suzanne Petitpierre. Her origin was a simple middle-class family in Lyons and she was desperately weary of the life her profession forced her to lead, the endless rounds of parties, dinners and theatres, as companion to film men, motor manufacturers, steel men, titled men, all of whom wished to be seen with the most beautiful and photographed model in the city. Mlle Petitpierre wanted nothing of any of them. She had no ambition for a career in films, or on the stage, or to marry a rich or titled man. What she desired more than anything else was somehow to be able to rejoin that middle class from which she had temporarily escaped, marry someone for love, some good, simple man, who was not too handsome or clever, settle down in a comfortable middle-class home and produce a great many little middle-class offspring. Such men existed she knew, men who were not consistently vain, boastful, or clever to the point where she could not keep up with them. But they were somehow now all outside of her orbit. Even at that very moment when she was beneath the

a town in France (*Lyon*).

gaze of many admiring eyes she felt lost and unhappy. She remembered vaguely having seen the young man who was regarding her so intensely, somewhere before, but could not place him.

Finally, Mrs. Harris of 5, Willis Gardens, Battersea, London, came bustling up the staircase already crowded with people to be received by Mme Colbert. And then and there an astonishing thing took place.

For to the regular clients and those who know, the staircase at Christian Dior's is a humiliating place. It was reserved strictly for the foolish, the merely curious, unimportant people and the minor press.

Mme Colbert regarded Mrs. Harris standing there in all her cheap clothing, and she looked right through them and saw only the gallant woman and sister beneath. She reflected upon the simplicity and the courage that had led her thither in pursuit of a dream, the wholly feminine yearning for an out-of-reach bit of finery, the touching desire, once in her dull cheerless life, to possess the ultimate in a creation. And she felt that somehow Mrs. Harris was quite the most important and worthwhile person in the gathering there of chattering females waiting to view the collection that day.

'No,' she said to Mrs. Harris. 'Not on the staircase. I will not have it. Come, I have a seat for you inside.'

She threaded Mrs. Harris through the throng, holding her by the hand and took her into the main salon where all but two of the gold chairs in the double rows were occupied. Mme Colbert always kept one or two seats in

remember who or what he was.
I will not allow it.

46

reserve for the possible unexpected arrival of some V.I.P., or a favoured customer bringing a friend.

She led Mrs. Harris across the floor and seated her on a vacant chair in the front row. 'There,' said Mme Colbert. 'You will be able to see everything from here. Have you your invitation? Here is a little pencil. When the models enter, the girl at the door will call out the name and number of the dress – in English. Write down the numbers of the ones you like the best, and I will see you afterwards.'

Mrs. Harris settled herself noisily and comfortably on the grey and gold chair. Her handbag she placed on the vacant seat at her left, the card and pencil she prepared for action. Then with a pleased and happy smile she began taking stock of her neighbours, who, although she had no means of identifying them, represented the highest society of the whole world.

The seat to Mrs. Harris's right was occupied by a fierce-looking old gentleman with snow-white hair and eyes which were of a penetrating blue and astonishingly alert and young looking. In the top buttonhole of his dark jacket was fastened what seemed to Mrs. Harris to be a small rosebud which both fascinated and startled her, since she had never seen a gentleman wearing any such thing before and so she was caught by him staring at it.

The keen blue eyes examined her closely, but the voice that addressed her in perfect English was dry and tired. 'Is there something wrong, madam?'

The thought that she might have been rude disturbed Mrs. Harris. 'Fancy me staring at you like that,' she apologised, 'where are my manners? I thought that was a rose in your buttonhole. Good idea too.' Then in explanation she added – 'I'm very fond of flowers.'

47

'Are you,' said the gentleman. 'That is good.' Whatever hostility had been caused by her stare was driven away by the pleasing innocence of her reply. He looked upon his neighbour with a new interest and saw now that she was a most extraordinary creature and one he could not immediately place. 'Perhaps,' he added, 'it would be better if this were indeed a rose instead of a – rosette.'

Mrs. Harris did not understand this remark at all, but the pleasant manner in which it had been delivered showed her that she had been forgiven for her rudeness. 'Isn't it lovely here?' she said by way of keeping the conversation going.

'Ah, you feel the atmosphere too.' Puzzled, the old gentleman was racking his brain, trying to catch or connect with something that was stirring there, something that seemed to be connected vaguely with his youth and his education which had been finished by two years at an English University. He was remembering the two dark and gloomy English college rooms that had been his bedroom and study, cold and bare, opening off a dark hallway, and strangely, as the picture formed in his mind, there was a pail standing in the hall at the head of the stairs.

Mrs. Harris's alert little eyes now dared to engage those of the old gentleman. They penetrated the fierceness of his exterior, to a warmth that she felt within. She wondered what he was doing there unaccompanied. Probably looking for a dress for his daughter or grand-daughter, she thought and, as always, with her kind, resorted to the direct question to satisfy her curiosity.

'Are you looking for a dress for your daughter?' Mrs. Harris enquired.

The old man shook his head, for his children were scattered and far removed. 'No,' he replied, 'I come here from time to time because I like to see beautiful clothes and beautiful women. It refreshes me and makes me feel young again.'

Mrs. Harris nodded assent. 'No doubt about that!' she agreed. Then with the pleasant feeling that she had found someone else in whom she might confide she leaned towards him and whispered: 'I've come all the way from London to buy myself a Dior dress.'

A flash of understanding illuminated the old gentleman, and he knew now who and what she was. The old picture of the dark hallway, and stairs with the pail at the top, returned, but now a figure stood beside the bucket, a large, untidy woman in a work-stained apron and large shoes, surrounded by brooms, mops, dusters and brushes. She had been for him the only cheerful note throughout the gloomy college rooms. He remembered that her name had been Mrs. Maddox, but to him and another French boy in the college she had always been Madame Mops, and as such had been their friend, counsellor, source of gossip and college news.

He remembered too that beneath the cheerful and comic exterior he had recognised the fearless bravery of women who lived lives of hardship and ceaseless toil to render their simple duties to their fellows. He could see her again now, as she charred the college. He could almost hear her speak again. And then he realised that he *had*. For seated next to him in the most exclusive dress salon in Paris, was the image of his Madame Mops of half a century ago.

True there was no physical resemblance, for his neighbour was slight and worn thin by work – the old gentleman's eyes dropping to her hands confirmed the guess –

49

but that was not how he recognised her; it was by the bearing, the speech, of course, and the sharp little eyes, but above all by the air of courage and independence that surrounded her.

'A Dior dress,' he echoed her – 'a splendid idea. Let us hope that you will find here this afternoon what you desire.'

There was no need in him to question her as to *how* it was possible for her to fulfil such a wish. He knew from his own experience something of the nature of these special Englishwomen and simply assumed that she had been left a large sum of money, or had won a football pool. But had he known just how Mrs. Harris had come by the entire sum needed to satisfy her ambition he would not have been surprised either.

They now understood one another as did old friends who had much in life behind them.

'I wouldn't tell anyone else,' Mrs. Harris confessed from the comfort of her new-found friendship, 'but I was frightened to death to come here.'

The old man looked at her in astonishment – 'You? Frightened?'

'Well,' Mrs. Harris confided, 'you know the French. . . .'

The gentleman sighed, 'Ah yes. I know them very well. Still there is nothing now but for you to choose the gown that you like the best. It is said the collection this spring is wonderful.'

There was a stir and a rustle. A smart, expensively-dressed woman came in attended by two sales ladies and made her way to the seat beside Mrs. Harris where the brown handbag containing the latter's fortune reposed momentarily.

Mrs. Harris snatched it away with an 'Oops, dearie, sorry!' then brushed the seat of the chair with her hand and smiling cheerily said: 'There you are now. All ready for you.'

The woman who had close-set eyes and a too small mouth sat down with a rattle of gold bracelets and immediately Mrs. Harris found herself in a cloud of the most beautiful and intoxicating perfume. She leaned closer to the woman for a better sniff and said with sincere admiration: 'Ooh, you do smell good.'

The newcomer made an annoyed motion of withdrawal and a line appeared between the narrow eyes. She was looking towards the door as though searching for someone. And then she found whom she sought – Madame Colbert, and she beckoned her over, speaking sharply and loudly to her in French as she neared: 'What do you mean by seating a vulgar creature like this next to me? I wish her removed at once. I have a friend coming later who will occupy her chair.'

Mme Colbert's heart sank. She knew the woman and the breed. She bought not for love of clothes, but for the show of it. Nevertheless she spent money. To gain time Mme Colbert said: 'I am sorry, madame, but I have no recollection of reserving this seat for a friend of yours, but I will look.'

'It is not necessary to look. I told you I wished this seat for a friend. Do as I say at once. You must be out of your mind to place such a person next to me.'

The old gentleman next to Mrs. Harris was beginning to colour, the crimson rising from the neckline of his collar and spreading to his ears. His blue eyes were turning as frosty as his white hair.

For a moment Mme Colbert was tempted. Surely the little cleaning woman from London would understand if she explained to her that there had been an error in the reservations and the seat was taken. She would be able to see just as much from the head of the stairs. Her glance travelled to Mrs. Harris sitting there in her shabby coat and absurd hat. And the object of this argument not understanding a word of the conversation looked up at her with her sunniest and most trusting smile. 'Aren't you a dear to put me here with all these nice people,' she said, 'I couldn't be happier if I was a millionaire.'

A worried-looking man appeared at the head of the salon. The angry woman called to him: 'Monsieur Armand, come here at once; I wish to speak to you. Mme Colbert has sat me next to this dreadful woman. Am I forced to put up with this?'

Confused by the vehemence of the attack, M. Armand took one look at Mrs. Harris and then to Mme Colbert he made secret pushing movements with his hands, and said: 'Well, well. You heard. Get rid of her at once.'

The angry red in the face of the fierce old gentleman turned to purple, he half rose from his chair, his mouth opening to speak when Mme Colbert preceded him.

Many thoughts and fears had raced through the Frenchwoman's mind, her job, the reputation of the company, possible loss of a wealthy client, consequences of defiance of authority. Yet she also knew that though M. Armand was her superior, on this floor she was in supreme command. And now that the unsuspecting Mrs. Harris was the subject of a cruel attack the manageress experienced more than ever the feeling of kinship and sisterhood with this strange

to put up with = to suffer, endure.

53

visitor from across the Channel returning overpoweringly. Whatever happened, move her she could not and would not. It would be like beating an innocent child. She thrust out her firm round chin at M. Armand and declared: 'Madame has every right to be seated there. She has journeyed here from London especially to buy a dress. If you wish her removed, do it yourself, for I will not.'

The old gentleman resumed both his seat and his normal colour, but he was staring at Mme Colbert, his face lit up with a kind of fierce and angry joy. He had momentarily forgotten Mrs. Harris in his admiration of this French-woman of selfless courage, honour and honesty.

As for M. Armand, he hesitated – and was lost. Some of Dior's best clients, he was aware, were frequently most odd-appearing and peculiar women. Mme Colbert was supposed to know what she was doing. Throwing up his hands in a gesture of surrender, he fled the battlefield.

The woman snapped: 'You will hear further about this. I think, Mme Colbert, this will cost you your position,' got up and marched from the room.

'Ah, but I think it will not!' The speaker was now the old gentleman with the white hair, fierce look and rosette of the Légion d'Honneur in his buttonhole. He arose and declared somewhat dramatically: 'I am proud to have been a witness that the spirit of true democracy is not entirely dead in France and that decency and honour still have some supporters. If there are any difficulties over this I will speak to the Patron myself.'

Mme Colbert glanced at him and murmured: 'Monsieur

'He who hesitates is lost' is a saying meaning that a person who does not act quickly loses his chance to act.

the head of the House of Dior.

54

is very kind.' She was bewildered, sick at heart and not a little frightened, as she peered momentarily into the dark unknown future – Jules passed over again, a broken man, she dismissed from her job.

A girl stationed at the door called out: 'Number one, "Nocturne",' as the first model walked into the room.

A little shriek of excitement was torn from Mrs. Harris. 'It's begun!'

In spite of her state of mind Mme Colbert felt suddenly a strange flooding up in her of love for the charwoman and bending over her she gave her a little squeeze. 'Look well, now,' she said, 'so that you may recognise your heart's desire.'

Chapter 7

Thereafter, for the next hour and a half, before the fascinated eyes of Mrs. Harris, some ten models paraded one hundred and twenty specimens of the highest dressmaker's art to be found in the world.

It was not long before Mrs. Harris began to become accustomed to this bewildering display of richness and finery and soon came to recognise the various models upon their appearance in turn. And among them, of course, there was the one and only Natasha, the star. It was the custom in the salon to applaud when a creation made a particular hit, and Mrs. Harris's palms, hard from application to scrubbing brush and mop, led the appreciation each time Natasha appeared looking lovelier than the last. Once, during one of her appearances, the charwoman noticed a tall, blond, pale young man standing outside, staring hungrily as Natasha made an entrance and said to herself: 'Coo, he's in love with her, he is. . . .'

She was in love herself, was Mrs. Harris, with Natasha, with Mme Colbert, but above all with life and the wonderful thing it had become. The back of her card was already covered with pencilled numbers of frocks and dresses and notes, messages and reminders to herself that she would never be able to read. How could one choose between them all?

And then Natasha glided into the salon wearing an

when a dress was felt to be a special success.

evening gown, Number 89, called 'Temptation'. Mrs. Harris had just an instant in which to note the enchanted expression on the face of the young man by the door before he turned away quickly as though that was what he had come for, and then it was all up with her. She was lost, dazzled, blinded, overwhelmed by the beauty of the creation. This was *it*!! Thereafter there were yet to come further wonderful examples of evening gowns until the traditional appearance of the bridal costume brought the show to a close, but the char saw none of them. Her choice was made. Feverish excitement accelerated her heartbeat. Desire ran like fire in her veins.

'Temptation' was a black velvet gown, floor length, covered half-way from the bottom up with a unique design picked out in beads of jet that gave to the skirt weight and movement. The top was a mass of cream, delicate pink and white chiffon, and lace from which arose the ivory shoulders and neck and dreamy-eyed dark head of Natasha.

Rarely had a creation been better named. The wearer appeared like Venus arising from the pearly sea, and likewise she presented the attractive figure of a woman emerging from disordered bedclothes. Never had the upper portion of the female form been more alluringly framed.

The salon burst into immediate applause at Natasha's appearance and the clapping of Mrs. Harris's palms sounded like the beating upon boards with a broomstick.

Cries and murmurs arose on all sides from the males present while the fierce old gentleman thumped his walking stick upon the floor and beamed with pleasure. The garment covered Natasha most decently and morally and yet was wholly indecent and overwhelmingly alluring.

she was overcome, finished.

57

Mrs. Harris was not aware that there was anything extra-ordinary as to the choice she had made. For she was and eternally would be a woman. She had been young once and in love. She had had a husband to whom her young heart had gone out and to whom she had wished to give and be everything. Life in that sense had not passed her by. He had been shy, embarrassed, tongue-tied, yet she had heard the love words forced haltingly from his lips whispered into her ear.

The bridal model showed herself quickly; the gathering emerged from the salon towards the grand staircase where the sales women waited for their customers.

Mrs. Harris, her small blue eyes glittering, found Mme Colbert. 'Number eighty-nine, Temptation,' she cried, and then added, ' oh Lord, I hope it doesn't cost more than I've got.'

Mme Colbert smiled a thin, sad smile. She might almost have guessed it. 'Temptation' was a poem created in materials by a poet of women, for a young girl in celebra-tion of her freshness and beauty and awakening to the mysterious power of her sex. It was invariably demanded by the faded, the middle-aged women. 'Come,' she said, ' we will go to the back and I will have it brought to you.'

She led her through grey doors into another part of the building, until at last Mrs. Harris found herself in a curtained-off cubicle on a corridor that seemed to be part of an endless succession of similar corridors and cubicles. Each cubicle held a woman, like a queen bee in a cell, and through the corridors rushed the worker bees with the honey – armfuls of garments, to present them where they had been ordered for trial and further inspection.

unable to say what one wants to say.

Here, attended by sales-women, needlewomen, cutters, fitters and designers, who hovered about them with measures, scissors, needle and thread and mouths full of pins, rich French women, rich American women, rich German women, rich South American women, titled women from England and from India, and even it was rumoured a wife or two from Russia, spent their afternoons – and their husbands' money.

And here too, in the midst of this thrilling and enchanting hive, surrounded by her own attendants, stood the London charwoman, clothed in 'Temptation' – whom it fitted astonishingly, yet logically, since she too was slender, thinned by occupational exercise and too little food.

She issued from the wondrous foam of sea-shell pink, sea-cream and pearl-white like – Ada Harris from Battersea. The creation worked no miracles except in her soul. The thin neck and greying head that emerged from the gown, the weathered skin, small bright blue eyes and apple cheeks contrasted with the classic beauty of the black velvet panels were absurd – but still, not wholly so, for the beautiful gown as well as the radiance of the person in it yet managed to lend an odd kind of dignity to this extraordinary figure.

For Mrs. Harris had attained her Paradise. She was in a state of dreamed-of and longed-for bliss. All of the hardships, the sacrifices, the economies and hungers and doings-without she had undergone faded into unimportance. Buying a Paris dress was surely the most wonderful thing that could happen to a woman.

Mme Colbert was consulting a list. 'Ah, yes,' she murmured, 'the price is five hundred thousand francs.' The apple cheeks of Mrs. Harris paled at this announcement.

There was not that much money in the whole world. 'That is five hundred English pounds,' Mme Colbert continued, 'which is one t' ousand four hundred American dollars, and with our little reduction for cash – '

Mrs. Harris's yell of triumph interrupted her 'That's exactly what I've got. I'll have it! Can I pay for it now?' and she reached for her purse.

'Of course – if you wish. But I do not like to handle such an amount of cash. I will ask M. Fauvel to descend.'

A few minutes later, the young, blond M. André Fauvel appeared in the cubicle, where Mrs. Harris recognised him at once as the man who had gazed with such a hopelessly loving expression upon Natasha.

'It's all here, dearie,' she said. 'Fourteen hundred dollars, and that's my last penny.' And she handed him the bundle of dollars.

'It doesn't need altering,' Mrs. Harris went on. 'I'll take it just as it is. Have it wrapped for me.'

Mme Colbert smiled. 'But my dear, surely you must know we cannot let you have *this* dress. This is the model and there is yet another month of summer showings. We will make you one, of course, exactly like – '

Alarm squeezed the heart of Mrs. Harris as the import of what Mme Colbert was saying struck her. 'What! Make me one – ' she repeated, and suddenly looking much older than she was, asked, 'How long does it take?'

Mme Colbert felt alarm now too: 'Ten days to two weeks ordinarily – but for you we would make an exception and rush it through in a week – '

The awful silence following upon this revelation was broken by the cry torn from the depth of Mrs. Harris – 'But don't you understand? I can't stay in Paris. I've just enough money to get me home! It means I can't have it!' She saw herself back in the gloomy Battersea flat, empty-handed, possessed only of her useless money. What did she want with all that money? It was the ownership of 'Temptation' for which she craved, body and soul, even though she never again put it on her back.

Thereupon, to the horror of all, they saw two tears form at the corner of her eyes, followed by others that ran down the red-veined cheeks as Mrs. Harris stood there in the midst of them, in the exquisite gown, miserable, abandoned, desperately unhappy.

And M. André Fauvel, accountant and money-man, supposedly with heart of stone suddenly felt himself moved as he had never thought possible, deeply and unbearably touched; and he knew that it was the hopeless love he felt for the girl Natasha whose sweet and dear body had inhabited this garment that had brought him so suddenly to an understanding of the tragedy of this stranger who, on the point of realising her greatest desire, was to suffer disappointment.

Thereupon he dedicated his next remark to that girl who would never know how much or greatly he had loved her, or that he had loved her at all for that matter. He presented himself to Mrs. Harris with a formal little bow: 'If madame would care, I invite her to come to my home and remain with me during this period as my guest. It is not much – only a small house, but my sister has had to go to Lille and there would be room –'

His reward was almost immediate in the expression that came over the little woman's face and her cry of 'Oh bless you. Do you really mean it?' and the odd gesture of Mme Colbert which might have been the brushing away of something from the corner of her eyes as she said – 'Oh André, you are an angel!'

But then Mrs. Harris gave a little shriek, 'Oh dear – my jobs – '

'Haven't you a friend,' suggested Mme Colbert helpfully, 'someone who would help you out while you were away?'

'Mrs. Butterfield,' Mrs. Harris replied immediately '– but a whole week – '

'If she is a real friend she will not mind,' Mme Colbert counselled. 'We could send her a telegram from you.'

Mrs. Butterfield would not mind, particularly when she heard about it all, Mrs. Harris felt certain. Her conscience smote her when she thought of Pamela Penrose and her important producer friends and her career. Yet there was 'Temptation'. 'I'll do it,' she cried. 'I've got to have it.'

Thereupon, to her excitement and delight, *her* crowd of fitters, cutters, dressmakers and needlewomen descended upon her with measures, pins, thread, scissors and all the wondrous exciting things that were connected with making up the most expensive dress in the world.

By late afternoon, when at last Mrs. Harris was done with measuring and fitting, the most remote corner of the establishment had heard the tale of the London charwoman who had saved her wages and journeyed to Paris to buy herself a Dior dress. Members of the staff from the lowest to the highest, including the Patron himself, had managed an excuse to pass by the cubicle to catch a glimpse of this remarkable Englishwoman.

And later, while for the last time Mrs. Harris was dressed in the model, Natasha herself, about to start out on a round of evening's engagements, came and saw nothing unusual or absurd in the figure of the charwoman in the beautiful creation, for she had heard the story and felt herself touched by it. She understood Mrs. Harris. 'I am so glad you have chosen that one,' she said simply.

When the latter suddenly said – 'Oh! However am I going to get to this Mr. Fauvel? He gave me his address, but I wouldn't know where it was –' Natasha was the first to offer to take her thither.

'I have a little car; I will drive you there myself. Let me see where it is.'

Mrs. Harris handed her the card M. Fauvel had given her with the address. Natasha wrinkled her pretty forehead over the name. 'Monsieur André Fauvel,' she repeated. 'Now where have I seen that name before?'

Madame Colbert smiled – 'It is only the accountant of our company, my dear,' she said, 'he is the one who pays out your salary.'

'Well!' laughed Natasha – 'One might love such a one. Very well, Madame Harris, when you are ready I will take you to him.'

Chapter 8

Thus it was that, shortly after six, Mrs. Harris found herself
in Natasha's little car, bound for the home of M. Fauvel
When they rang the doorbell, M. Fauvel cried: '*Entrez
entrez* – come in,' from within, believing it to be Mrs
Harris by herself. They pushed through the door and
found themselves in a home in exactly that state of chaos
to be expected when a bachelor's sister has gone away.

Dust lay thick; nothing had been touched for a week
books and clothes were scattered about. It took no trick of
the imagination to estimate the piled-up dishes in the
kitchen sink, the greasy pans on the stove, as well as the
condition of the bathroom and the unmade beds above.

Never was a man in such confusion. His face crimson
with shame, M. Fauvel appeared before them stammering
'Oh, no – no – Mademoiselle Natasha – you of all people
– I cannot permit you to enter – I, who would have given
anything to have welcomed – I mean, I have been living
alone here for a week – I am disgraced – '

Mrs. Harris saw nothing unusual in the condition of the
place, for it was exactly the same as greeted her in every
house, flat or room when she came to work daily in London

'Here, here, dearie,' she called out genially. 'What's all
the fuss about? I'll have all this put right in a moment
Just you show me where the mop cupboard is, and get me a
bucket and a brush – '

it was not difficult to estimate in the imagination.

As for Natasha – she was looking right through and past the dirt and disorder to the solid middle-class furniture she saw beneath it. She saw comfort without elegance – and her heart yearned towards it. This was a home, and she had not been in one like it since she had left her own in Lyons.

'Oh please,' she cried, 'may I remain and help? Would you permit it, monsieur?'

M. Fauvel went into a stream of apologies – 'But mademoiselle – you of all people – in this pigsty, for which I could die of shame – to spoil those little hands – never in a thousand years could I permit – '

'Ow – come off it, dearie,' ordered Mrs. Harris. 'Can't you see the girl *wants* to? Run along now and keep out of the way and let us get at it.'

Dear me, Mrs. Harris thought to herself as she and Natasha put on aprons and seized upon brooms and dust-cloths, *French people are just like anyone else, plain and kind, only maybe a little dirtier. Now who would have thought it after all one hears?*

That particular evening, Natasha had an invitation for drinks with a count, an appointment for dinner with a duke, and a late evening engagement with an important politician. It gave her the most intense pleasure she had known since she came to Paris to leave the count standing and, with the professional and efficient Mrs. Harris, make the dirt fly in that house, as it had never flown before.

It seemed no time at all before everything was in order again. The furniture gleamed, the beds were stiff with clean sheets and pillowcases, the ring around the bath banished pots, pans, dishes, glasses and knives and forks washed up

stop being foolish (slang).
to fail to keep her appointment with the count.

Oh, it is good to be inside a home again, where one can be a woman and not just a silly little doll. Natasha said to herself as she attacked the dust in the corners. And she found herself suddenly touched by the plight of M. Fauvel and thought, *That must be a fine sister he has, poor boy, and he is so ashamed* – and suddenly in her mind's eye she saw herself holding this blond head with the blushing face to her breast while she murmured, 'Now, now, my little one, do not worry. Now that I am here everything will be all right again.' And this to a perfect stranger she had seen only vaguely before as he appeared occasionally in the background of the establishment for which she worked. She stood quite still for a moment with astonishment at herself, leaning upon her broom, the very picture of housewifely grace, to be discovered so by the sudden return of the enchanted M. Fauvel himself.

So busy had been the two women that neither had noticed the absence of the accountant until he suddenly reappeared with a mountain of parcels.

'I thought that after such exhausting labours you might be hungry – ' he explained. Then, regarding an untidy, dirty, but thoroughly contented Natasha, he stammered: 'Would you – could – dare I hope that you might remain?'

The count and his invitation were already gone from her mind. Now the duke and the politician joined him. With the utmost simplicity and naturalness, and quite forgetting herself, Natasha, or rather Mlle Petitpierre of Lyons, threw her arms about M. Fauvel's neck and kissed him. 'But you are an angel to have thought of this, André. I am so hungry. First I will allow myself a bath, and then we will eat and eat and eat.'

M. Fauvel thought too that he had never been so happy

in his life. What an astonishing turn things had taken ever since – why, ever since that wonderful little Englishwoman had come to Dior's to buy herself a dress.

Mrs. Harris ate for the week before, for this and the next as well. There had never been a meal like it before and probably never would again. Her eyes gleamed with delight.

'The night outside is heavenly,' said M. Fauvel, his eyes meltingly upon the sweet, contented face of Natasha, 'perhaps afterwards we will let Paris show herself to us – '

'Ooof!' grunted Mrs. Harris, filled with good food. 'You two go. I've had a day to end all days. I'll just stay home here and wash the dishes and then get into my bed and try not to wake up back in Battersea.'

But now, a feeling of restraint and embarrassment seemed suddenly to descend upon the two young people and Mrs. Harris in her state of fullness failed to notice it. Had his guest consented to go, M. Fauvel was thinking, all would have been different and the high spirits of the party plus the glorious presence of Natasha might have been maintained. But, of course, without this extraordinary person the thought of his showing Dior's star model the sights of Paris suddenly seemed utterly ridiculous.

To Natasha, Paris at night was the interior of a series of expensive nightclubs, of which she was heartily sick. She would have given much to have stood under the starry night and looked out over these stars reflected in the sea of the lights of Paris – and in particular with M. Fauvel at her side.

But with Mrs. Harris's deciding to go to bed there seemed no further excuse for her presence. She had already intruded too much into his privacy. She had shamelessly

heartily sick = completely tired.

68

examined his home with broom and duster, seen the neglect in his sink, permitted herself the almost unthinkable intimacy of washing out his bath, and in her high spirits, the even more unpardonable one of bathing in it herself.

She became suddenly overcome with confusion, and blushing murmured: 'Oh, no, no, no. I cannot, it is impossible. I am afraid I have an appointment. I must be going.'

M. Fauvel accepted the blow which he expected. *Ah, yes,* he thought, *you must return, little butterfly, to the life you love best. Some count, duke, or even prince will be waiting for you. But at least I have had this one night of bliss and I should be content.* Aloud he murmured, 'Yes, yes, of course, Mademoiselle has been too kind.'

He bowed, they touched hands lightly and their glances met and for a moment lingered. And this time the sharp knowing eyes of Mrs. Harris understood: *Oho,* she said to herself, *so that's how it is. I should have gone with them.*

But it was too late to do anything about it now and the fact was that she really was too full to move. 'Well, good night, dears,' she said loudly and pointedly, and tramped up the stairs, hoping that with her presence removed they might still get together on an evening out. But a moment later she heard the front door opened and shut and then the clatter as the motor of Natasha's car came to life. Thus ended Mrs. Ada Harris's first day in a foreign land and among a foreign people.

The following morning, however, when M. Fauvel proposed that in the evening he show her something of Paris, Mrs. Harris lost no time in suggesting that Natasha be included in the party. M. Fauvel protested that sightseeing was not for such exalted creatures as Mlle Natasha.

'Nonsense,' said Mrs Harris. 'What makes you think she's different from any other young girl when there is a handsome man about? She'd have gone with you last night if you had had the brains to ask her. You just tell her I said she was to come.'

That morning the two of them encountered briefly upon the grey carpeted stairs at Dior. They paused for an instant uncomfortably. M. Fauvel managed to stammer: 'Tonight I shall be showing Mrs. Harris something of Paris. She has begged that you would accompany us.'

'Oh,' murmured Natasha, 'Madame Harris has asked? She wishes it? Only she?'

M. Fauvel could only nod dumbly. How could he on the grand staircase of the House of Christian Dior cry out 'Ah, no, it is I who wish it, crave it, desire it, with all my being. It is I who worship the very carpet on which you stand.'

Natasha finally said: 'If she desires it then, I will come. She is adorable, that little woman.'

'At eight then.'

'I will be there.'

They continued on their routes, he up, she down.

The enchanted night at last took place. It began for the three of them with a ride up the Seine on a boat to a river-side restaurant in a tiny suburb. With a wonderful sense of feeling M. Fauvel avoided those places where Mrs. Harris might have felt uncomfortable, the expensive luxury places, and never knew how happy Natasha herself felt in this more modest environment.

From that time on, unspoken, the nightly gathering of the three for roamings about Paris became taken for granted.

taken for granted = accepted as natural and usual.

In the daytime, while they worked, except for her fittings which took place at eleven-thirty in the mornings, and her tidying of Fauvel's house, Mrs. Harris was free to explore the city on her own, but the evenings were heralded by the arrival of Natasha in her car, and they would be off.

Thus Mrs. Harris saw Paris. And in this manner, Mrs. Harris lost all fear of the great capital, for they showed her a life and a city full of her own kind of people – simple, rough, realistic and hard-working and engaged all of them in the same kind of struggle to get along as she herself back home.

Chapter 9

Free to wander where she would during the day in Paris except for her fittings, Mrs. Harris never quite knew where her footsteps would lead her. She explored thus the Left Bank and the Right and eventually through accident stumbled upon a certain paradise in the middle, the Flower Market located by the Quai de la Corse on the Île de la Cité.

Never in her life had she found herself in the midst of such an intoxicating wealth of blossoms of every kind, colour and shape. Here were streets that were nothing but a mass of plants in pots, plants in pink, white, red, purple, mingling with huge bunches of cream, crimson and yellow flowers. There were many plants and flowers Mrs. Harris did not even know the name of, and, of course, row upon row of Mrs. Harris's own very dearest potted geraniums. All the beauty that she had ever really known in her life until she saw the Dior dress had been flowers. Now, from every quarter came beautiful scents and through this richness of colour and scent Mrs. Harris wandered as if in a dream.

Yet another and familiar figure was wandering in that same dream, none other than the fierce old gentleman who had been Mrs. Harris's neighbour at the Dior show and whose name was the Marquis de Chassagne, of an ancient

the Left and Right Banks of the River Seine.
the island in the River Seine in the city of Paris.

72

family. There was no fierceness in his face now and he seemed at peace as he strolled through the lanes of fresh blossoms and breathed deeply and with satisfaction of the perfumes that mounted from them.

His path crossed that of the charwoman, a smile broke out over his countenance and he raised his hat with the same gesture he would have employed raising it to a queen. 'Ah,' he said, 'our neighbour from London who likes flowers. So you have found your way here.'

Mrs. Harris said: 'It's like a bit of heaven, isn't it? I wouldn't have believed it if I hadn't seen it with my own eyes.'

'And the dress you came here to seek. Did you find it?' enquired the marquis.

Mrs. Harris grinned like a naughty little girl. 'Didn't I just! It's the one called "Temptation", remember? It's black velvet trimmed with black beads and the top is some sort of pink soft stuff.'

The marquis reflected for a moment and then nodded: 'Ah, yes, I do remember it was worn by that exquisite young creature.'

'Natasha,' Mrs. Harris concluded for him. 'She's my friend. It's being made for me, I've got three more days to wait.'

'And so, with infinite good sense, you acquaint yourself with the genuine attractions of our city.'

'And you - ' Mrs. Harris began and broke off in the middle of the sentence, for suddenly she knew the answer to the question she had been about to ask.

But the Marquis de Chassagne was not at all put out and

Didn't I just = I certainly did!
put out = disturbed.

73

only remarked gravely: 'You have guessed it. There is so little time left for me to enjoy the beauties of the earth. Come, let us sit on this seat in the sun, a little, you and I, and talk.'

They sat then, side by side on the green wooden bench, in the midst of the colours and perfumes, the aristocrat and the charwoman, and conversed. They were worlds apart in everything but the simplicity of their humanity, and so they were really not apart at all. For all his title and eminent position, the marquis was a lonely widower, his children married and scattered. And what was Mrs. Harris but an equally lonely widow, but with the courage to set out upon one great adventure to satisfy her own craving for beauty and elegance. They had much in common these two.

The marquis returned to a subject that had interested him. 'And you say that Mademoiselle Natasha has become your friend?'

'She's a dear,' said Mrs. Harris, 'not at all like you might expect, high and mighty with all the fuss that's made over her. She's as unspoiled as your own daughter would be. They're all my friends, I do believe – that nice young Monsieur Fauvel, the cashier, – it's his house I am stopping at – and that poor Mme Colbert – '

'Eh,' said the marquis, 'and who is Madame Colbert?'

It was Mrs. Harris's turn to look surprised. 'Oh, surely you know Madame Colbert – the manageress – the one who tells you whether you can come in or not. She's a real love. Imagine putting Ada Harris right in with all the rich people.'

'Ah, yes,' said the marquis with renewed interest,

For all = in spite of.

'that one. A rare person, a woman of courage. But why poor?'

Mrs. Harris settled more comfortably into the bench to enjoy a good gossip. Why, this French gentleman was just like anybody else back home when it came to interest in other people's trouble and miseries. Her voice became happily confidential as she tapped him on the arm and answered: 'Oh, but of course, you wouldn't know about her poor husband.'

'Oh,' said the marquis, 'she has a husband then? What is the difficulty, is he ill?'

'Not exactly,' replied Mrs. Harris. 'Twenty-five years in the same office – the brains of his office he is. But every time he comes up for a big job they give it to some count or some rich man's son until his heart is near broken and Madame Colbert's too. There's another chance for him now and no one to speak up for him or give him a hand. Madame Colbert's crying her poor dear eyes out.'

A little smile that was almost boyish illuminated the stern mouth of the old marquis. 'Would Madame Colbert's husband by any chance have the name of Jules?'

Mrs. Harris stared at him in blank amazement, as though he were a magician. 'Go on!' she cried, 'how did *you* know? That's his name, Jules, do you know him? Madame Colbert says he's got more brains in his little finger than all the rest of them in their heads.'

The marquis suppressed a chuckle and said: 'Madame Colbert may be right. There can be no question as to the intelligence of a man who has the good sense to marry such a woman.' He sat in silent thought for a moment and then from an inside pocket produced a card and wrote on

give him a hand = help him.

the back a brief message with an old-fashioned fountain pen. He waved the card dry and then presented it to Mrs. Harris. 'Will you remember to give this to Madame Colbert the next time you see her.'

Mrs. Harris inspected the card with unashamed interest. The printed side read 'Le Marquis Hypolite de Chassagne, Conseiller Extraordinaire au Ministère des Affaires Etrangères, Quai d'Orsay,' which meant nothing to her except that her friend was an important person with a title. She turned it over, but the message was in French and she did not understand that either. 'Right,' she said, 'I won't forget.'

During Mrs. Harris's fitting that morning Mme Colbert came into the cubicle to see how things were going. 'Here,' said Mrs. Harris, 'he said I was to give you this.' She produced the card and handed it to Mme Colbert.

The manageress turned first red and then deathly pale as she examined the card and the message on the reverse. The fingers holding the card began to shake. 'Where did you get this?' she whispered. 'Who gave it to you?'

Mrs. Harris looked concerned. 'The old gentleman. The one that was sitting next to me with the red thing in his buttonhole that day at the collection. I met him in the Flower Market and had a bit of a chat with him. It isn't bad news, is it?'

'Oh, no, no,' murmured Mme Colbert, her voice trembling with emotion and hardly able to hold back the tears. Suddenly she went to Mrs. Harris, took her in her arms and held her tightly for a moment. 'Oh, you wonderful, wonderful woman,' she cried, and then turned and fled

The Foreign Office.

from the cubicle. She went into another booth, an empty one, where she could be alone to put her head down upon her arms and cry unashamedly with the joy of the message which had read: 'Please ask your husband to come to see me tomorrow. I may be able to help him – Chassagne.'

Chapter 10

On the last night of Mrs. Harris's magical stay in Paris, M. Fauvel had planned a wonderful party for her and Natasha, an evening out with dinner at the famous 'Pré-Catalan' in the Bois de Boulogne. Here, with gay music in the background, they were to feast on the most delicious and luxurious of foods and drink the finest wines that M. Fauvel could procure.

And yet, what should have been the happiest of times for the three started out as an evening of peculiar and penetrating sadness.

M. Fauvel looked distinguished and handsome. Natasha had never looked more beautiful in an evening dress of pink, grey and black, cut to show off her sweet shoulders and exquisite back. Mrs. Harris came as she was except for a fresh lace blouse she had bought with some of her remaining English pounds.

Her sadness was only a faint shadow on the delight and excitement of the place and the hour and the most thrilling thing of all that was to happen tomorrow. It was due to the fact that all good things must come to an end and that she must be leaving these people of whom in a short time she had grown so extraordinarily fond.

But the unhappiness that gripped M. Fauvel and Mlle Petitpierre was of heavier, gloomier and thicker stuff. Each had reached the conclusion that, once Mrs. Harris departed, this magic which had brought them together and

79

thrown them for a week into one another's company would be at an end.

Natasha was no stranger to the 'Pré Catalan'. Countless times she had been taken there to dine and dance by wealthy admirers who meant nothing to her. There was only one person now she wished to dance with ever again, who she desired to hold her close, and this was the unhappy-looking young man who sat opposite her and did not offer to do so.

In spite of the night, the lights, the stars and the music, M. Fauvel and Mlle Petitpierre were in danger of passing one another by.

For as he gazed upon the girl, his eyes misty with love, M. Fauvel knew that this was the proper setting for Natasha – here she belonged among the light-hearted and the wealthy. She was not for him. He had never been to this colourful restaurant before in the course of the modest life he led and he was now more than ever convinced that it was only because of Madame Harris that Natasha endured him. He was aware that a curious affection had grown up between that lovely creature, Dior's star model, and the little cleaning woman. But then he had grown very fond of Mrs. Harris himself. There was something about this Englishwoman that seemed to drive straight to the heart.

As for Natasha, she felt herself pushed out of André Fauvel's life by the very thing for which she so much yearned, his middle-class respectability. He would never dream of marrying one such as her, presumably spoiled by expensive clothes and too much publicity. No, never. He would choose some good, simple, middle-class daughter of a friend, or acquaintance, or perhaps his absent sister would choose her for him. He would settle down to the tranquillity of an unexciting married life and raise many children. How she wished that she could be that wife and lead that tranquil life by his side and bear for him those children!

The band beat out a lively dance. A bottle of wine stood opened on the table. All about them voices were raised in merriment and laughter, and the three sat enveloped in thick silence.

Shaking off the shadow that had fallen across her and feeling the wonderful excitement of life and beauty that was all about them, Mrs. Harris suddenly became aware of the condition of her two companions and tried to do something about it. 'Aren't you two going to dance?' she asked.

M. Fauvel blushed and muttered something about not having danced for a long time. He would have loved nothing better, but he had no wish to compel Natasha to endure an embrace that must be unpleasant to her.

'I do not feel like dancing,' said Mlle Petitpierre. She would have given everything to have been on the floor with him at that moment, but would not embarrass him after his obvious reluctance to have anything to do with her beyond the normal requirements of duty and politeness.

But Mrs. Harris's keen ears had already caught the hollowness of their voices with the unmistakable note of misery contained therein, and her shrewd eyes darted from one to the other, searchingly.

'Look here,' she said, 'what's the matter with you two?'

'But nothing.'

'Of course, nothing.'

In their efforts to prove this M. Fauvel and Mlle Petitpierre both at the same moment broke into bright and meaningless chatter aimed at Mrs. Harris while they avoided one another's eyes and which they kept up for a minute until it suddenly stopped and the silence resettled itself more thickly.

'Oh dear,' said Mrs. Harris, 'of all the fools, me. I thought you two had it settled between you long ago.' She turned to M. Fauvel and asked: 'Haven't you got a tongue in your head? What are you waiting for?'

M. Fauvel blushed crimson. 'But – but – I – I – ' he stammered, 'she would never '

Mrs. Harris turned to Natasha. 'Can't you help him a bit? In my day when a young lady had her heart set on a fellow she'd let him know soon enough. How do you think I got my own husband?'

There was a white light above the beautiful dark, head of the girl, and now she turned as pale as the light.

'But André does not – ' she whispered.

'Nonsense!' said Mrs. Harris. 'He does – and so do you. I've got eyes in my head. You're both in love. What's keeping you apart?'

At the same moment M. Fauvel and Mlle Petitpierre began:

'He wouldn't – '

'She couldn't – '

Mrs Harris chuckled. 'You're in love, aren't you? Who can't do what?'

For the first time the two young people looked one another directly in the eyes and saw what lay there. Caught up in one another's gaze, they saw at last the expressions of hope and love. Two tears formed at the corners of Natasha's exquisite eyes and glistened there.

'And now, you must excuse me for a minute,' Mrs.

among all the fools there are, I am the most foolish.

82

Harris announced significantly. She arose and went off in the direction of the Ladies' Room.

When she returned a good fifteen minutes later, Natasha was locked in M. Fauvel's arms on the dance floor, her head pillowed on his chest and her face was wet with tears. But when they saw she had returned to the table, they came running to her and threw their arms about her. M. Fauvel kissed one withered apple cheek, Natasha the other, and then the girl put both arms around Mrs. Harris's neck and wept there for a moment murmuring: 'My dear, I am so happy, André and I are going to – '

'Are you really?' said Mrs. Harris. 'What a surprise! How about some wine to celebrate?'

They all lifted their glasses and thereafter it was the gayest, brightest, happiest night that Mrs. Harris had ever known in her whole life.

83

And so the day dawned at last when 'Temptation' was finished and it came time for Mrs. Harris to take possession of her treasure wrapped in piles of soft paper and packed in a lovely cardboard box with the name 'Dior' printed on it in golden letters.

There was quite a little gathering for her in the Salon of Dior's in the late morning – she was leaving on an afternoon plane – and from somewhere a bottle of wine had appeared. Mme Colbert was there, Natasha and M. Fauvel, and all of the fitters, cutters and needlewomen who had worked so hard and faithfully to finish her dress in record time.

They drank her health and safe journey, and there were gifts for her, a genuine leather handbag from a grateful Mme Colbert, a wrist watch from an equally grateful M. Fauvel and gloves and perfume from the more than grateful Natasha.

The manageress took Mrs. Harris in her arms, held her closely for a moment, kissed her and whispered in her ear: 'You have been very lucky for me, my dear. Soon perhaps I shall be able to write to you of a big announcement concerning my husband.'

Natasha hugged her too and said: 'I shall never forget you, or that I shall owe all my happiness to you. André and I will marry in the autumn.'

M. André Fauvel kissed her on the cheek and fussed over

her, advising her to take care of herself on the return trip, and then with the true concern of a man whose business is with cash asked: 'You are sure now that you have your money to pay the duty in a safe place? You have it well hidden away, no? It is better not to have it in the purse where it might be snatched.'

Mrs. Harris grinned her wonderful grin. Well fed for the first time in her life, rested and happy she looked younger by years. She opened her new leather handbag to show the air-ticket and passport therein, with one single green pound note, a five hundred franc note and a few left-over French coins to see her to the airport. 'That's the lot,' she said. 'But it's plenty to get me back to my duties. There's nothing for anyone to snatch.'

'Oh la la! But no!' cried M. Fauvel, his voice shaken by sudden anguish while a fearful silence fell upon the group in the salon as the shadow of threatening disaster made itself felt. 'I mean the customs duty at the British airport. Mon Dieu! Have you not provided? At thirty pence in the pound' – he made a swift calculation – 'that would be one hundred and fifty pounds. Did you not know you must pay this?'

Mrs. Harris looked at him stunned – and looked twenty years older. 'Oh!' she whispered, 'a hundred and fifty pounds? I've got *one*! Ow, why didn't somebody tell me? How was I to know?'

Mme Colbert reacted fiercely. 'La, what nonsense are you talking, André? Why pay duty any more to customs? You think those titled ladies and rich Americans do? They all smuggle, and you too, my little Ada, shall smuggle yours – '

thirty pence duty for each pound the dress is worth.

The little blue eyes of Mrs. Harris became filled with fear, alarm, suspicion. 'That would be telling a lie, wouldn't it?' she said, looking helplessly from one to the other – 'I don't mind telling a fib or two, but I don't tell lies. That would be breaking the law. I could go to jail for that.' Then as the true and ghastly import of what M. Fauvel said dawned upon her she quite suddenly sank down on to the grey carpet, covered her face with her workworn hands and sent up a wail of despair that penetrated through the establishment so that the *Great Patron* himself came running in. 'I can't have it. It isn't for such as me. I should have known my place. Take it away – give it away, do anything. I'll go home and forget about it.'

The story of the difficulty ran through the building. Experts appeared from all sides to give advice. It was the *Patron* himself, familiar with Mrs. Harris's story, who solved the problem with one swift generous stroke – or thought he had. 'Reduce the price of the dress to this good woman,' he ordered accountant Fauvel, 'and give her the balance in cash to pay the duty.'

'But sir,' protested the horrified Fauvel, who now for the first time himself saw the trap into which Mrs. Harris had fallen, 'it is impossible!'

They all stared at him as though he were a poisonous snake. 'Do you not see? Madame has already unintentionally broken British law by exporting the one thousand four hundred dollars, illegally exchanged by her American friend in the United Kingdom. If now she, poor woman, appeared at the British customs at the airport declaring a dress worth five hundred pounds and offered a further hundred and fifty pounds in cash to pay the duty, there would be enquiries how she, a British subject, had come by these monies; there would be a scandal – '

They continued to look at the unfortunate accountant as though he were a snake, but they also knew that he was right.

' Let me go home and die,' wailed Mrs. Harris.

Natasha was at her side, her arms about her. Voices rose in a flood of sympathy. Mme Colbert had an inspiration. ' Wait,' she cried, ' I have it.' She, too, dropped to her knees at Mrs Harris's side – ' My dear, will you listen to me? I can help you. I shall be lucky for you, as you have been for me – '

Mrs. Harris removed her hands to reveal the face of an old and frightened woman. ' I won't do anything dishonest – or tell any lies.'

' No, no. Trust me. You shall say nothing but the absolute truth. But you must do exactly how and what I say for, my dear, we *all* wish you to have your beautiful dress to take home. Now listen.' And Mme Colbert, placing her lips close to Mrs. Harris's ear so that no one else might hear, whispered her instructions.

As she stood in the customs hall of London Airport, Mrs. Harris felt sure that her thumping heart must be heard by all, yet by the time the pleasant-looking young customs officer reached her, her natural courage and cheerfulness buoyed her up, and her naughty eyes were even twinkling with an odd kind of pleasure.

On the counter before her rested, not the beautiful Dior box, but a large and well-worn suitcase of the cheapest kind.

I have it = I have the solution to this problem.

The officer handed her a card on which was printed the list of dutiable articles purchased abroad.

'You read it to me, dearie,' Mrs. Harris grinned at him, 'I left my glasses at home.'

The inspector glanced at her sharply once to see whether he was being fooled, the pink rose on the green hat waved at him: he recognised the breed at once. 'Hallo,' he smiled. 'What have *you* been doing over in Paris?'

'Having a bit of a holiday on my own.'

The customs man grinned. This was a new one on him. The British char abroad. The mop and broom business must be good, he reflected, then enquired in a routine manner, 'Bring anything back with you?'

Mrs. Harris grinned at him. 'Haven't I just? A genuine Dior dress called "Temptation" in my bag here. Five hundred pounds it cost. How's that?'

The inspector laughed. It was not the first time he had encountered the London char's sense of humour. 'You'll look very beautiful in it, I'm sure,' he said, and made a mark with a piece of chalk on the side of the case. Then he strolled off and presented his card to the next passenger whose luggage was ready.

Mrs. Harris picked up her bag and walked – not ran, though it was a great effort not to rush – to the door and out to freedom. She was filled not only with a sense of relief, but righteousness as well. She had told the truth. If, as Mme Colbert had said, the customs officer chose not to believe her, that was not her fault.

This was something he had never heard of before.
Haven't I just = I certainly have.

Chapter 12

Thus it was that at four o'clock in the afternoon of a lovely London spring day, the last obstacle overcome, and with 'Temptation' safely in her possession, Mrs. Harris found herself standing outside Waterloo Air Station, home at last. And but one thing was troubling her conscience. It was the little matter of Miss Pamela Penrose, the actress and her flat.

Her other clients were all wealthy, but Miss Penrose was poor and struggling. What if Mrs. Butterfield hadn't coped properly? It was still early. The keys to the flat were in her new handbag, now emerged from the suitcase. Mrs. Harris said to herself: 'Poor dear. It's early yet. Maybe she's got to entertain some important guests. I'll just call at her flat and surprise her by tidying up a bit.' She caught the proper bus and shortly afterwards was at the flat, inserting her key in the door.

No sooner had she the street door open, when the sound of the girl's sobs reached her, causing Mrs. Harris to hurry up the stairs and into the tiny living room, where she came upon Miss Penrose lying face down upon her couch crying her eyes out.

Mrs. Harris went to her, laid a sympathetic hand upon a shaking shoulder and said: 'Now, now, dearie, what's the matter? It can't be as bad as all that. If you're in trouble maybe I can help you.'

Miss Penrose sat up. '*You* help me!' she repeated, looking

through tear-swollen eyes. Then in a more kindly tone she said: 'Oh, it's you, Mrs. Harris. Nobody in the world could help me. Oh, I could die. If you must know, I've been invited to dine at the Caprice with Mr. Korngold the producer. It's my one and only chance to impress him and get ahead. Nearly *all* of Mr. Korngold's friends have become stars – '

'Well, now, I don't see anything to cry about there,' declared Mrs. Harris. 'You ought to be a star, I'm sure.'

Miss Penrose's grief turned momentarily to rage: 'Oh, don't be *stupid!*' she stormed. 'Don't you see? I can't go. I haven't anything to wear. My one good dress is at the cleaners and my other one has a stain. Mr. Korngold is frightfully particular about what the girls he takes out wear.'

Could you, had you been Mrs. Harris, with what she had in her suitcase, have been able to resist the temptation to play the good fairy? Particularly if you were still under the spell of the sweet gentleness and simplicity of Natasha, and the kindness of Mme Colbert and all their people, and knew what it was like to want something dreadfully, something you did not think you were ever going to get?

Before Mrs. Harris quite realised what she was saying, the words came out – 'See here. Maybe I can help you after all. I could lend you my Dior dress.'

'Your *what*? Oh, you – you horrible creature. How *dare* you make fun of me?' Miss Penrose's small mouth was twisted and her eyes cloudy with rage.

'But I'm not! It's true! I've just come back from Paris

frightfully particular = very difficult to please.
to play the good fairy = to give a person what he wants, as if by magic.

where I bought myself a Dior dress. I'd let you wear it tonight if it would help you with Mr. Korngold.'

Somehow Miss Penrose, once Miss Snite, brought herself under control as some instinct warned her that with these charwomen one never really knew what to expect. She said: 'I'm sorry. I didn't mean – but of course you couldn't – where is it?'

'Here,' said Mrs. Harris, and opened the suitcase. The intense gasp of wonder and excitement and the joy that came into the girl's eyes made it worth the gesture. 'Oh – oh – oh!' she cried. 'I can't *believe* it.' In an instant she had the dress out of its wrappings, holding it up, then hugging it to her she searched out the label with greedy fingers – 'Oh! it really *is* a Dior. May I try it on, Mrs. Harris? We are about the same size, aren't we? Oh, I could die with excitement.'

In a moment she was taking off her clothes, Mrs. Harris was helping her into the dress and a few minutes later it was again fulfilling the destiny for which it had been designed. With her lovely bare shoulders and blonde head rising from the chiffon Miss Penrose was both Venus appearing from the sea and Miss Snite emerging from the bedclothes.

Mrs. Harris and the girl gazed silently at the image reflected from the full-length mirror on the wall. The actress said: 'Oh you are a dear to let me wear it. I'll be ever so careful. You don't *know* what it means to me.'

But Mrs. Harris knew very well. And it seemed almost as though fate wished this beautiful creation to be worn and shown off and not hung away in a wardrobe. This being so, she had a request: 'Would you mind very much if I came to the restaurant where you are having dinner and stood outside to watch you go in? Of course, I wouldn't speak to you or anything – '

Miss Penrose said graciously: 'Of course I wouldn't mind. If you'll be standing at the right side of the door as I get out of Mr. Korngold's Rolls Royce, I can turn to you so that you can see me better.'

'Oh,' said Mrs. Harris. 'You *are* kind, dearie.' And meant it.

Miss Penrose kept her promise, or half kept it, for a storm came up and suddenly it was a thundery, rainy night when at half-past nine Mr. Korngold's Rolls Royce drew up at the entrance to the Caprice. Mrs. Harris was standing to the right of the door, somewhat protected from the rain by the wall of the building. Miss Penrose paused for one instant, turning towards Mrs. Harris. Then with a toss of her golden hair she ran swiftly into the doorway. Mrs. Harris had had no more than a glimpse of jet beads, a flash of foamy pink, white cream chiffon, and then it was over.

But she was quite happy and remained there a little longer, contented and lost in imaginings. For now the head waiter would be bowing low to *her* dress and leading *it* to a favoured and conspicuous table. Every woman in the room would recognise it at once as one from Dior; all heads would be turning as the creation moved through the aisles of tables, the velvet skirt, heavy with jet beads swinging perfectly, while above, the sweet, young bosom, shoulders, arms and pink and white face emerged from the lovely chiffon. Mr. Korngold would be pleased and proud and would surely decide to give so well dressed and beautiful a girl an important part in his next play.

And no one there, except the girl herself, would know that the exquisite gown which had done it all and had made every eye brighten with envy or admiration was the sole and exclusive property of Mrs. Ada Harris, char, of No. 5, Willis Gardens, Battersea.

And thither she went now smiling to herself all the way during the long bus ride home. There remained only the problem of Mrs. Butterfield, who would be anxiously awaiting her, to be dealt with. She would wish to see the dress, of course, and hear all about it. For some reason she could not understand, Mrs. Harris felt that she did not care for Mrs. Butterfield to know that she had lent her dress to the actress.

But by the time she had arrived at her destination she had the solution. A little fib and the fatigue that had collected in her bones would help her to avoid her friend's questions. 'Oh dear!' she said from the depths of Mrs. Butterfield's bosom where she found herself embraced; 'I'm so tired that I've got to hold my eyes open with my fingers. It's so late, I won't even stay for a cup of tea.'

'You poor dear,' sympathised Mrs. Butterfield, 'I won't keep you You can show me the dress – '

'It's coming tomorrow,' Mrs. Harris half-fibbed. 'I'll tell you all about it then.'

Once more in her own bed, she gave herself up to the sweet delicious sense of accomplishment and with not so much as a single fear as to what tomorrow might bring was soon fast asleep.

Chapter 13

The hour that Mrs. Harris devoted to Miss Penrose was from five to six, and all the next day, as she worked in the various homes of her other clients she lived in excited anticipation of that moment. At last it came and she hurried to the little flat and, opening the door, stood for a moment at the foot of the narrow staircase.

At first it was only disappointment that she experienced, for the place was dark and silent. Mrs. Harris would have liked to have heard from the girl's own lips the story of the triumph scored by the Dior dress and its effect upon Mr. Korngold.

But it was the strange, unfamiliar smell that assailed her nostrils that turned her cold with alarm and set the skin of her scalp pricking with terror. At the top of the stairs, Mrs. Harris turned on the lights in the living-room and went in. The next instant she was staring down, frozen with horror at the ruins of her dress. And then she knew what the odour was that had assailed her nostrils.

The Dior dress had been tossed carelessly upon the disordered couch with the burned-out velvet panel where the fire had eaten into it showing shockingly in a fearful gap of melted beadwork and burned cloth.

Beside it lay a pound and a hastily written note. Mrs. Harris's fingers were trembling so that she could hardly read it at first, but at last its contents became clear.

Dear Mrs. Harris, I am terribly sorry I could not stay

to explain in person, but I have to go away for a little while. I am most awfully sorry about what happened to the dress, but it wasn't my fault and if Mr. Korngold had not been so quick I might have burned to death. He said I had a very narrow escape. After dinner we went to a night club where I stopped to comb my hair in front of a mirror and there was an electric fire right underneath, and all of a sudden I was burning – I mean the dress, and I could have burned to death. I am sure they will be able to repair it and your insurance will take care of the damage, which is not as bad as it looks as it is only the one panel. I am going away for the week. Please look after the flat as usual. I am leaving a pound for your wages in the meantime.'

It was astonishing that when Mrs. Harris had finished reading the letter she did not cry out, or even murmur or say anything at all. Instead she took up the damaged garment, and, folding it carefully, packed it once more into the old suitcase Mme Colbert had given her and which she brought from the closet where she had put it the night before. She left the letter and the money lying on the couch, went downstairs and into the street. When she had closed the outside door, she paused only long enough to remove the key to the flat from her chain, since she would not be needing it any more, and push it through the letter box. Then she caught a bus for home.

It was damp and chilly in her flat. She put the kettle on for tea and then, guided by habit, she did all the things she was used to doing, even to eating, though she hardly knew what food she tasted. She washed up the dishes and put everything away. But there the mechanism ended and she turned to the unpacking of the ruins of the Dior dress.

She fingered the burned edges of the velvet and the

burned and melted jet. She knew night clubs, for she had cleaned in them. She thought she could see it happening – the girl, half-drunk, coming down the stairs from the street, on the arm of her escort, thoughtless, heedless of all but that which concerned herself, pausing before the first mirror to study herself and apply a comb.

Then the sudden ascent of smoke from her feet, the little shriek of fright, perhaps an orange line of fire in the dress and the man beating at it with his hands until it was extinguished and only the wreck of the most beautiful and expensive frock in the world remained.

And there it was in her hands now, still with the smell of burned cloth rising from it and which all the perfume given to her by Natasha would not suffice to blot out. A thing, once as perfect and beautiful as human hands could make it, was destroyed.

She tried to tell herself that it was not the fault of the girl, that it had been an accident and that only she herself was to blame for trying to play the good fairy to this spoiled child and bad actress who had not even. the grace to be grateful to her for her foolish gesture.

Mrs. Harris was a sensible person, a realist who had lived a hard life and did not deceive herself. Looking now upon this burned and tragic wreck of her desires she was well aware of her own foolish pride and vanity, not only involved in the possession of such a treasure, but in the displaying of it.

She had looked forward to the casual way she might say to her landlady, when questioned as to where she had been : ' Oh I was only over in Paris dearie, to look at the collection and buy myself a Dior dress. It's called "Temptation".' And, of course, she had imagined a hundred times the reaction of Mrs. Butterfield when she unveiled her prize. There would be no calling in of her friend now – or anyone else – for she would only say: 'Didn't I tell you something awful would happen? Things like that aren't for people like us! What were you going to do with it, anyway?'

What indeed had she been meaning to do with it? Hang it away in an old dark cupboard next to her aprons, and one poor Sunday frock, secretly to gaze at it when she came home at night? The dress had not been designed and created to be wasted in the dark of a cupboard. It was meant to be out where there were gaiety, lights, music and admiring eyes.

Quite suddenly she could not bear to look upon it any longer. She was at the end of her resistance to grief. She pushed it into the old suitcase, hurriedly blotting out the sight of it with the soft paper and then, flinging herself upon her bed, buried her face in her pillow and commenced to cry. She wept silently, after the fashion of women whose hearts have been broken.

She wept for her own foolishness, and too for her self-acknowledged guilt of the sin of pride and the swift, sure punishment that had followed; but mostly she wept simply and miserably for her lost dress and the destruction of this so dear possession.

She might have wept thus into eternity, but for the insistent ringing of her door bell which at last penetrated grief and into her consciousness. She raised her tear-swollen face momentarily and then decided to ignore it. It could be none other than Mrs. Butterfield, eager to see and discuss her Paris dress and hear of her adventures. What was there

unveiled her prize = displayed her treasure, the dress.

to show her now for the long wait, the hard work, the sacrifice and the foolish determination? A burned-out rag. Worse than Mrs. Butterfield's 'I told you so' would be the sympathy that would follow, and the warm but clumsy attempts to comfort her and which Mrs. Harris felt she could not bear. She wanted only to get on with her crying – to be allowed to weep alone until she died.

She pulled the damp pillow about her ears to shut out the sound of ringing, but now, somewhat to her alarm, heard it replaced by a loud knocking and thumping on the door, something rather more strenuous and commanding than she could connect with Mrs. Butterfield. Perhaps there was something wrong somewhere, an emergency, and she was needed. She arose quickly, brushed the hair out of her eyes and opened the door to reveal a BEA messenger standing there looking at her as though he had seen a ghost.

'Mrs. Harris, is it?' he asked weakly.

'Who else did you expect? Princess Margaret? Banging and thumping like that as if the house was on fire . . .'

'Phew!' he said, wiping his brow with relief, 'you gave me a fright, you did. I thought maybe you were dead. You not answering the doorbell, and these flowers to deliver. I thought they might be for the body.'

'Eh?' Mrs. Harris asked. 'What flowers?'

The messenger grinned. 'Flown over special from France, and express delivery. Here now. Leave the door open while I bring them in.'

Swinging wide the rear doors of the van he began to produce them, white box, upon long white box marked: '*Air Express – Perishable*'. It seemed to the mystified Mrs. Harris that he would never end his trips from the van to her living-room and that there must be some mistake.

But there was none. 'Sign here,' he said, his task at last ended, and putting his book under her nose. It was her name and address right enough – Madame Ada Harris, 5, Willis Gardens, Battersea.

He left and she was alone again. Then she turned to opening her boxes and packages and in an instant found herself transported back to Paris again, for the dull little room suddenly vanished beneath the garden of flowers that overwhelmed it, dark, deep red roses by the dozen, cream white lilies, bunches of pink and yellow flowers, buds ready to burst into every colour from deep blue to palest lemon. There were blooms of white and crimson, geraniums, bundles of sweet-smelling flowers and one great bunch of violets a foot across.

In an instant, her dwelling seemed changed into a stall of the *Marché aux Fleurs*, for, market-fresh, the crisp smooth flowers were still dewed with pearls of water.

Was this coincidence, or some magic foresight that this sweet, healing gift should reach her in her moment of deepest anguish? She detached the cards from the blossoms and read the messages on them. They were a welcome home, an outpouring of remembrance and affection from her friends, mixed with good news.

'Welcome home. We could not wait. André and I were married today. God bless you. Natasha.'

'I am the happiest man in the world thanks to you. André Fauvel.'

'A welcome back to the lady who loves flowers. Hypolite de Chassagne.'

'Compliments of M. Christian Dior' (this with the violets).

'Greetings on your return. The Staff of Christian Dior.'

'Good luck to you. Cutters, Fitters and Needlewomen Maison Christian Dior.'

And finally: 'Jules was named First Secretary of the Department for Anglo-Saxon Relations at the Quai d'Orsay today. What can I say, my dear, but thank you. Claudine Colbert.'

Her knees trembling beneath her, Mrs. Harris sank to the floor, leaned her cheek against the tight, smooth, cool, heavily fragrant roses Mme Colbert had sent her, tears filling her eyes again, her mind flooded with memories by the messages, the colours and the fragrance of the flowers that filled her little living-room.

Once again she saw the understanding, womanly Mme Colbert, with her dark shining hair and pure skin, the exquisite, laughing Natasha and the blond, serious-minded, grave-faced M. Fauvel who overnight had changed from an adding machine into a boy and a lover.

All manner of memories and pictures crowded into her thoughts. For an instant she saw the wrinkled brows and concentrated expressions of the fitters kneeling before her, their mouths bristling with pins. She felt once more the thick, grey carpet beneath her feet and smelled the sweet, thrilling scent of the interior of the House of Dior.

The noise and murmur of the voices of the audience and patrons in the grey and white salon seemed to come back to her, and immediately, blinking through her tears she was there again as each model more beautiful than the last clad in the loveliest frocks, suits and gowns came thrusting, swaying or gliding into the room.

From there it was but a flash for her to be back in the hive of the cubicles, a part of the delicious atmosphere of woman's world compounded of the rustle of silks and satins, the many perfumes carried thither by the clients, the murmuring voices of sales-women and dressmakers like the buzzing of bees and the sound of whispering from neighbouring booths and smothered laughter.

Then she was sitting in the sunlight beneath a sky of a peculiar blue, on a bench in the Flower Market surrounded by nature's own fashion creations, flowers in their matchless shapes and colours and offering perfumes of their own. And next to her was a handsome aristocratic old gentleman who had understood her and treated her as an equal.

But it was the people she had met who kept returning to her thoughts and she remembered the expression on the faces of Fauvel and Natasha as they had embraced her the night of the 'Pré-Catalan' and seemed to feel once again the warm pressure of Mme Colbert's arms about her as she had kissed her before her departure and whispered: 'You have been very lucky for me, my dear – '

Reflecting now upon Mme Colbert, Mrs. Harris thought how the Frenchwoman had worked and schemed to help her to realise her vain, foolish wish to possess a Dior dress. Had it not been for her and her clever plan at the end it would never have reached England. And Mrs. Harris thought that even the damage to Temptation' might not be irreparable. A letter to Mme Colbert would result in the immediate dispatch of another beaded panel such as had been destroyed. A clever needlewoman could insert it so that the dress would be as good as new. And yet, would it ever be the same again?

This question had a most curious effect upon Mrs. Harris. It stopped the flow of tears from her eyes and brought her to her feet once more as she looked about the flower-laden room and the answer came to her in one shrewd, inspired burst of understanding.

It would not. It would never be the same again. But then neither would she.

For it had not been a dress she had bought so much as an adventure and an experience that would last her to the end of her days. She would never again feel lonely, or unwanted. She had ventured into a foreign country and a foreign people whom she had been taught to suspect and despise. She had found them to be warm and human, men and women for whom human love and understanding were at the heart of life. They had made her feel that they loved her for herself.

Mrs. Harris opened the suitcase and took out 'Temptation'. Once more she fingered the burnt place and saw how easily the panel could be replaced and the damage repaired. But she would not have it so. She would keep it as it was, untouched by any other fingers than those which had hurried every stitch because of love and feeling for another woman's heart.

Mrs. Harris hugged the dress to her thin bosom, hugged it hard as though it were alive and human, holding her face to the soft folds of the material. Tears flowed again from the small, shrewd, blue eyes and ran down the apple cheeks, but they were no longer tears of misery.

She stood there holding and embracing her dress, and with it she was hugging them all, Madame Colbert, Natasha, André Fauvel, down to the last unknown worker, needlewoman and cutter, as well as the city that had bestowed upon her such a priceless memory, a treasure of understanding, friendship and humanity.

GLOSSARY

A

absurd: foolish, causing people to laugh.
accelerate: to make quicker.
accent: a way of speaking.
accountant: one who keeps accounts of money.
acknowledged: self-acknowledged=recognised and admitted by oneself.
adorable: very lovable.
adornment: something worn to make beautiful and ornament.
air: manner, appearance.
aisle: passage between rows of chairs, tables etc.
alert: watchful, fully awake.
alluringly: charmingly, attractively, temptingly.
alter: to change (of a dress—to make it fit).
amaze: to surprise greatly. n. amazement.
anguish: great sorrow and suffering.
ankle: joint between foot and leg.
annum: per annum (Latin)=a year.
anticipation: looking forward to something before it happens.
apology: statement of regret for doing wrong.
appalled: very frightened and shocked.
apron: loose garment to protect clothes (as worn by a servant).
aristocrat: a person of high birth or rank. adj. aristocratic.
ascend: to climb, go up. n. ascent=rising.
aspiring: hoping eagerly to realise an ambition.
assail: to attack.
assent: agreement.
astounded: greatly surprised.

B

bachelor: an unmarried man.
bang: to hit with a heavy, noisy blow.
banished: driven away.
bank-roll: the amount of money a person has in the bank.
BEA Viscount: a British European Airways airplane.

bead: small ball (made of wood, glass etc., here of JET) with hole through for string or cotton, used as ornament.

beam: to smile happily.

bearing: manner, way of behaving.

beast: person who behaves in an unpleasant way.

beckon: to make sign with the finger asking somebody to come.

beloved: very much loved.

bestow upon: to give.

bewildered: unable to understand properly and therefore worried. bewildering = causing one to feel bewildered.

bill: dollar bill = a dollar bank-note.

blink: blink through tears = to look unsteadily and with difficulty through tears.

bliss: perfect happiness.

blond(e): n. and adj. (person) having fair hair and skin.

blot out: make to disappear; destroy.

blouse: woman's outer garment worn on upper part of body.

blush: to become red in the face from confusion.

booth: a small enclosure with walls or curtains to make it private.

bosom: the human breast.

boutique: (French) shop.

brace: to support and hold firmly in place.

bracelet: band worn on the wrist or arm as an ornament.

brakes: mechanism which slows down a car's wheels.

breed: a certain kind of animal or person.

bristling: having many sharp points.

broom: a large brush on long handle for sweeping floors.

broomstick: the wooden handle of a BROOM.

buoy up: to keep up a person's spirits.

buoyancy: high spirits which prevent a person from sinking in difficulty.

bureau de change: office where money is changed.

bustle: n. noisy movement. v. to move quickly and excitedly.

butterfly: a beautiful insect that flies quickly here and there.

buzzing: sound made by bees.

C

cab: taxi (taxicab).

calculation: a working with numbers.

carpet: a large thick floor-covering. carpeted = covered with a carpet.

cartier: a well-known and very expensive jeweller's shop.

cashier: person in shop or office who has charge of the money.

casual: happening by chance, as if one did not care.

ceiling: the inside surface of the roof of a room.

chaos: complete confusion and lack of order.

char: n. (short for) charwoman, a woman employed by the hour or day to do house-cleaning. v. (i) to work as a charwoman (ii) to clean.

chat: a friendly talk about unimportant things.

chatter: quick foolish talk. adj. chattering.

cheerily: happily.

cherished: loved.

chiffon: very thin kind of cloth used in women's clothes.

chin: the part of the face below the mouth.

chorus: group of singers in a musical play.

chuckle: (to give) a quiet laugh.

cĭnema: building in which moving pictures are shown.

clad: dressed.

clapping: noise made by striking the hands together.

classic: simple and of excellent quality and taste:

clatter: a loud confused noise.

client: person who receives help from or does business with another.

closet: very small room or cupboard used for storing things.

clumsy: heavy and unskilful.

code: set of rules.

coincidence: something which happens, by chance, just at the right moment.

come by: obtain.

comic: causing people to laugh.

commence: begin.

compassion: feeling of pity for another's sorrows.

compliments: greetings.

compounded: made up of.

conceive: think, imagine.

concentrate: give one's whole mind to.

concerned: worried.

confide: trust and tell secrets to.

confidences: private matters, secrets.

confidential: as when telling a secret.

confirm: to make sure and prove correct.

consistently: always in the same way.

conspicuous: easily seen and attracting attention.

consult: to seek advice from.

converse: to talk together in a friendly way.

corridor: a long, narrow passage.

corruption: dishonesty.

costume: dress. bridal costume=the dress worn by a woman at her marriage.

couch: a long, low chair for sitting or lying.

counsel: to give advice. counsellor=person who gives advice.

count: a title of nobility.

countenance: the appearance and expression of the face.

counter: a long table.

countless: too many to be counted.

coupon: a printed paper. football POOL coupon=printed paper on which one writes down one's guesses of the results of football games to be played on the following Saturday.

cover: to protect and hide another's difficulty.

coveted: greatly desired.

crave: to have a great desire for. n. craving.

creation: something that is made, and, especially, a very expensive lady's dress.

crimson: deep red.

crisp: firm and fresh.

cubicle: a small enclosure divided off from a larger room.

currency: money.

customs duty: money paid on goods brought into a country. the customs = the building where goods are *inspected* and DUTY is paid.

D

dawn upon: begin to become clear and understood.

dazzled: made unable to see clearly by the brightness of something.

dearie: (slang) my dear.

decency: good behaviour and ideas. adj. decent.

decently: in a proper manner.

dedicate: to give, as if to a god.

defiance: disobedience and lack of respect.

defy: to set a problem that cannot be solved.

delicious: very delightful.

deserted: left empty of people.

despise: to look down on as low and worthless.

destination: the place to which one is going.

destiny: the purpose which fate has intended.

detach: to take off.

dieu: 'Mon Dieu!' = 'My God!' (French).

disaster: sudden great misfortune.

discarded: thrown away.

disgraced: shamed and dishonoured.

disillusionment: the destruction of one's dreams.

disordered: disarranged untidily.

dispatch: sending off.

dramatically: suddenly and excitingly like an event in a play.

draw: the result of a football match when both sides have the same score.

dreadfully: very much.

dripping: with small drops of water falling.

due: due north = straight towards the north.

dutiable: on which DUTY must be paid.

duty: money paid on goods brought into a country.

E

economies: ways of saving money.

ecstasy: a state of very great happiness.

elegant: having grace and beauty. n. elegance.

embarrassed: made to feel uncomfortable, not knowing what to say.

embassy: the offices which a government has in a foreign country.

emerge: to come out.

emergency: a sudden difficulty which makes quick action necessary.

eminent: high in rank or fame.

enchant: to put a magic charm on. enchantment=a state of magic charm.

engaged: busy.

engagements: social or business appointments.

entertain: entertain the possibility=consider the possibility.

envelop: to cover completely.

environment: surroundings.

escort: a man who accompanies a woman.

establishment: a set of persons and a building kept for a certain purpose, e.g. a
      home, a business.

eternity: time without end.

eventually: at last.

exalted: high, noble.

exclusive: kept apart for certain people only.

exhausting: very tiring, using up all one's strength.

explosion: a bursting open.

export: to take something out of one country to another.

express: very fast.

exquisite: very fine and beautiful.

exterior: the outside.

F

fantastic: unreal and impossible.

fascinate: to charm.

fatigue: tiredness.

fearfully: very much.

feminine: belonging to women. n. femininity.

fib: (to tell) a small, unimportant lie.

finery: beautiful clothes and ornaments.

finger-tip: the extreme end of the finger.

fitting: trying on a dress to see how well it fits.

fled: ran away (past tense of flee).

fling: to throw.

floor-to-ceiling: reaches from the floor to the CEILING.

flourish: to grow well in a healthy way.

flower-laden : loaded with flowers.

flush : flush of excitement=the first fresh moment of excitement.

foam : the white edge of a wave of the sea; something that is like this in appearance.

fog : dirty, cloud-like condition of the air (caused by dampness and smoke) making it difficult to see properly.

foresight : seeing what is going to happen in the future.

forlorn : cheerless, sad, without hope.

formula : a fixed form of words for a particular occasion.

fragrant : having a beautiful smell. n. fragrance.

frail : weak.

franc : a French coin.

frock : a woman's dress.

frog : a green and brown jumping creature that lives both on land and in water.

front : false front=false appearance put on to deceive.

frosty : cold and white. (frosty eyes=eyes cold with anger).

frown : to draw the skin round the eyes into folds as when displeased or worried.

fulfil : to complete.

fuss : unnecessary noise and excitement; to fuss over=to be very anxious that all is well. to kick up a fuss=to make trouble.

G

gallantry : bravery.

gamble : (to make) an arrangement to risk winning or losing money by guessing the result of a future event.

gasp : (to) struggle for breath e.g. when very surprised.

genially : in a pleasant cheerful manner.

genuine : real, true.

geranium : a flower, usually red, often grown in pots in the windows of houses.

gesture : a movement of the face or hands, or a deed used to express one's feelings.

ghastly : terrible.

gin : a strong drink.

glide : to move gently and quietly.

glisten : to shine.

gloomy : dark, with low spirits.

gossip : unimportant news usually spread by talking.

grave : serious.

grin : (to give) a wide smile.

grunt : to make noise like that of a pig.

guarantee : that which makes certain.

H

half-drunk : half way to being overcome by strong drink.

halt : a stop.

haltingly : hesitatingly and uncertainly.

hangings : curtains and long pieces of cloth hung on the walls of a room for decoration.

hardship : difficulty, lack of comfort.

headquarters : the chief place of business.

heartily : with much goodwill.

heedless : careless of, taking no thought.

heralded : begun.

hive : place where bees live, i.e. a busy place.

hoarsely : with a rough-sounding voice.

horrible : causing great fear and dislike.

horrid : unpleasant, unkind, selfish.

horrified : very worried and fearful.

hostile : unfriendly, acting like an enemy. n. hostility.

housewife : a married woman who is in charge of a house.

hover : to wait about in an uncertain manner.

hug : to press close to the body with one's arms.

humiliating : causing feelings of great shame.

humour : to make someone happy by giving what is wanted.

I

identification : way of proving what a place is.

identity : who and what a person is.

illegally : against the law.

illuminate : to give light to.

impersonal : not affecting one as an individual.

import : meaning.

imposing : fine, causing admiration.

infinite : without limits.

inhospitably : in an unfriendly manner towards one's guests.

initial : first.

insert : to put into.

inspect : to examine carefully. n. inspection.

inspector : an official whose work is to examine something carefully.

instinctively : with a natural inborn desire.

intensely : very sharply and carefully. adj. intense=very great and strong.

internal : inside.

intimacy : close familiarity.

intoxicating : causing excitement and loss of control (as when overcome by strong drink).

intrude: to enter without being invited or welcome.
irreparable: not able to be repaired.
irresistible: not able to be resisted.
ivory: the colour of the valuable long teeth of an elephant.

J

Jack: Union Jack=the flag of Great Britain.
jacket: a short coat.
jail: prison.
jerk: a sudden, sharp movement.
jet: hard black material used for ornament on dresses.

K

kettle: pot used for boiling water.
kinship: relationship, likeness.

L

label: small piece of cloth fixed to a dress on which is written the maker's name.
laden: loaded.
landing: level section between two parts of a staircase.
leavings: what is left over and not wanted.
leisure: leisure time=time when one is free from work.
let-down: disappointment.
likewise: in the same way; also.
linger: to stay as if unwilling to go away.
logically: according to reason.
lone: alone, by oneself.
longed-for: greatly desired.
longing: feeling of great desire.
love: an expression (slang) used to show friendliness.
luggage: baggage.

M

M.: short for Monsieur (French)=Mr.
maintain: to support something and make it continue.
Maison: Maison Christian Dior=the business house of Christian Dior (maison (French)=house).
marché aux fleurs (French) flower market.

marquis: a Frenchman of noble rank.

matchless: having no equal.

mean: ungenerous.

medium: the means by which something is done.

menacingly: threatening harm.

merriment: happiness.

mess: a state of dirt and disorder.

métro: the underground railway in Paris.

millionaire: a very rich man.

mingling: mixing.

minor: smaller, less important.

miracle: a wonderful event not according to laws of nature.

Mlle: short for Mademoiselle (French) = Miss.

Mme: short for Madame (French) = Mrs.

model: a woman who shows off dresses in a shop by wearing them. v. to show off a dress in this way.

momentarily: for a very short time.

mon dieu: My God! (French).

mop: (to work with) a long-handled tool used for cleaning floors.

motto: a saying used as a rule of life.

mound: a small hill.

mount: to climb.

mutter: to speak quietly without moving the lips very much.

mystified: unable to understand something mysterious.

N

nightclub: place of entertainment open until late at night for eating, drinking and dancing.

nocturne: belonging to the night (here used as a name for a dress).

nostrils: the two openings in the nose.

O

obscured: made dark, hidden from view.

obstacle: something that stands in one's way and causes difficulty.

obvious: clearly seen.

occupational: belonging to one's work.

odour: smell.

offspring: children.

orbit: the path in which one moves in life.

outrageousness: something extraordinary and shocking.

overnight: in the course of one night.

overpoweringly: too strongly to resist.
overwhelm: to overcome completely and swallow up.

P

pail: bucket.
palm: flat inside surface of the hand.
panel: one of the pieces with which a dress is made up.
parade: to walk past and show off.
paradise: heaven.
passport: a paper allowing one to enter a foreign country.
patron: (i). a regular customer.
          (ii). (French) the head of a business.
peak: the highest point.
penetrate: to enter into, pass through, find out.
penniless: without any money.
pension: widow's pension=money paid by state to a woman to help her live after death of her husband.
perfume: a pleasant-smelling liquid.
persist: to continue in spite of difficulty.
pigsties: (plural of) pigsty=a dirty untidy place like a hut in which a pig lives.
plight: difficult state.
plus: added to.
pool: football pool=competition in which each competitor pays a small amount of money and guesses the results of football matches. Those making the best guesses win large amounts of money.
precaution: care taken to prevent harm occurring.
precede: to go or act before somebody else.
prepared: ready, willing.
presumably: supposedly; taken as being true.
priceless: of very great value.
pricking: giving a sharp pain as if with a needle.
privacy: a person's own private life and affairs.
procure: to obtain.
producer: man in charge of the making of a film or play.
profess: to make a claim to.
pub: (short for public house) a place where strong drink is sold.
publicity: being made widely known.

Q

quarter: from every quarter=from every direction.
quiver: shake.

R

rack: (i). n. frame on which things are hung (as in a shop).

(ii). v. rack the brain=stretch and search the mind for a thought.

radiance: appearance of light and happiness.

rag: a bit of cloth.

rattle: noise caused by pieces of metal hitting together.

react: to act as the result of an act.

realist: n. one who sees things as they really are. adj. realistic.

recollection: memory.

refined: clear and of good quality.

reflect: to think. reflective=thoughtful.

refrigerator: machine which keeps food cold.

regard: to look at.

rejected: refused, turned away.

relieved: made different and not all the same.

reluctance: unwillingness.

remote: distant.

repose: to rest, lie on.

resort to: to go to, to turn to, to get what one wants.

respectability: good and proper behaviour.

restraint: holding back.

restriction: rule limiting one's actions.

resume: to return to.

revelation: something previously unknown which is revealed.

reverse: the back.

ridiculous: silly, laughable.

righteous: just and good.

roaming: wandering.

Rolls Royce: a very expensive make of car.

rosette: a small imitation rose worn by a Frenchman to whom a high honour (membership of the Légion d'Honneur) has been given.

rounds: course of events one following another.

routine: regular and normal.

rumoured: said in common talk and perhaps true or untrue.

rustle: noise as made when dead leaves, paper, stiff cloth are moved.

S

salon: a room in which guests, customers, are received.

satin: silk material of shiny appearance.

scalp: the skin of the head.

scandal: public talk and anger about a wrongdoing.

scarf: long piece of cloth worn about neck or head.

scold: to blame, find fault with.

scrub : to wash with a brush.

self-acknowledged : recognised and admitted by oneself.

self-indulgence : thinking too much of oneself and of one's own desires and troubles.

selfless : unselfish.

setting : surroundings.

sex : the condition of being male or female.

shabby : worn and old.

shattered : broken into small pieces.

sheer : complete and unspoiled by anything else.

shiver : to shake with cold or fear.

short : short answers = bad-tempered answers.

shrewd : sharp, keen in mind.

shriek : a high cry.

shrink : to make smaller.

shudder : a shaking of the body.

shy : not sure of oneself, easily frightened by other people.

sidewalk : footpath at side of a road.

significantly : with special meaning.

sink : container in kitchen in which dirty dishes are washed.

Sirius : a star.

sisterhood : feeling one woman has of being related to another because they have similar difficulties.

sixties : approaching her sixties = nearly 60 years of age.

slight : thin.

slipper : a light, loose shoe worn indoors.

smote : past tense of smite = to hit.

smothered : covered up.

smuggle : to take goods secretly in or out of a country, thus breaking the law.

snatch :   (i). to take quickly.
           (ii). to seize suddenly and steal.

sniff : to draw air into the nose and smell.

sole : only.

soothingly : in a calming way.

sparkling : flashing like a jewel.

specimen : an example.

speculation : guessing.

spell : magic influence.

spine : the backbone.

squeeze : to press tightly.

staggering : making one hesitate and fall as when hit.

stall : table from which goods are sold in a market.

stammer : to speak with difficulty, hesitatingly.

star : a very well-known person (e.g. actor or actress, model).

stern : serious and firm.

stifle : to try to stop in order to hide.

stitch : the small length of thread fixed into the cloth by one movement of the needle when sewing.

116

storm :   (i). to storm in = to come in excitedly like a storm.

           (ii). to storm at = to shout at and be angry with.

stout : strongly built, fat.

stoutly : strongly.

stray : to wander away from the proper path.

strenuous : using much strength.

stroll : to walk in an unhurried way.

study : room in which a person reads and writes.

stumble upon : to find by accident.

stunned : made senseless as if by a blow on the head.

substituting : working in place of another.

suburb : outlying part of a city.

suffice : to be enough.

suitcase : small case for clothes carried in a traveller's hand.

summing-up : a collection of the important facts in a few words.

suppress : to prevent, push down.

surpass : to go beyond and be better.

surrender : the act of yielding and saying one is beaten.

T

telegram : message sent by telegraph.

temporarily : for a short time.

thereafter : after that time.

therein : in that thing, in those things.

thereupon : immediately, afterwards.

thither : to that place.

throng : a crowd.

thumbing : turning over the pages of a book using the thumb.

thump : to beat heavily.

tragedy : a sad, ruinous event. adj. tragic.

tramp : to walk heavily.

tranquillity : calmness. adj. tranquil.

transported : carried.

treat : to pay for somebody else's pleasure or entertainment.

twinkling : flashing with light (like a star).

U

ultimate : furthest, last.

unbearably : in a way that it is impossible to bear.

underground : the underground railway in London.

Union Jack : the flag of Great Britain.

universe-shattering : breaking up into small pieces (shattering) all the sun, stars, the world (the universe).

unshed: unshed tears = tears which have not fallen.
unsuspecting: having no idea that trouble is approaching.
unthinkable: so shocking that one does not like to think about it.
utmost: greatest.
utterly: completely.

V

vacant: empty.
vaguely: not clearly or certainly.
vague-minded: not clear or certain in one's ideas.
van: a motor car for carrying goods.
vanity: emptiness, worthlessness.
Venus: the goddess of love who was born by rising from the sea.
very: that very instant = that exact instant.
v.i.p.: a very important person.
vivid: full of life.
vocabulary: the words a person uses.
vulgar: common, rough.

W

wail: (to give) a cry of grief.
wardrobe: cupboard in which clothes are hung.
waver: to move from one opinion to another and back again.
weathered: made rough by the weather.
widower: a man whose wife has died.
winnings: money won by a GAMBLE.
withered: dried up.
wondrous: causing great wonder.
worthwhile: of value and worthy of respect.
would-be: intending, wishing to be.
wrinkle: to make the skin go into small folds.

Y

yawn: opening the mouth to draw in breath when one is tired or *bored.*
yearn: to desire greatly.
yell: a loud cry.

Z

zip: (short for) zip-fastener = fastener for joining two pieces of cloth together.

THE BRIDGE SERIES

General Editor J A Bright